LONDON LINES
WITHDRAWN

DUE DATE

London Lines

THE CAPITAL BY UNDERGROUND

MICHAEL KELLY

MAINSTREAM
PUBLISHING

EDINBURGH AND LONDON

The moral right of the author has been asserted

First published in Great Britain in 1996 by
MAINSTREAM PUBLISHING COMPANY (EDINBURGH) LTD
7 Albany Street
Edinburgh EH1 3UG

Reprinted 1997

ISBN 1 85158 776 4

A catalogue record for this book is available from the British Library

Printed and bound in Finland by WSOY

DEDICATION
To Jordan who will soon be able to travel with me

CONTENTS

ACKNOWLEDGMENTS

Thanks to Mike Stanger for all his input, research and support. Thanks, too to Tom, Kate and Jane Kinninmont for putting me up so many times and for so much sound literary advice. David and Liz Smith supplied me with many quirky London anecdotes, some of which seem to have a basis in fact. David Ellis and Tricia Austin allowed me access to the London Transport Library and archives and gave valuable advice.

The extract on page 62 from *Metroland* is reproduced by permission of Desmond Elliott the Administrator of the Estate of Sir John Betjeman.

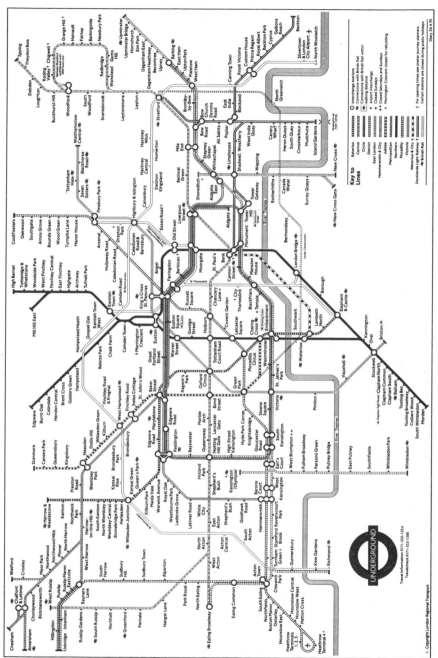

© **London Transport**

Diary 2A 4 95

CHAPTER ONE

VICTORY UNDERGROUND

The fiftieth anniversary of VE-Day was one I wanted to celebrate in London.

I had seen the old footage of cheerful Londoners defiantly trudging down the stairs of the tube stations to muck in together safely underground, while Goering's bombers plastered the city. So I guessed the Tube would be playing its part in the festivities planned for 6-8 May 1995.

As a war baby myself, London seemed to be the only place where the full flavour of the victory could be tasted. But what could I actually do? Join the official party in Hyde Park? Nothing very novel there. And would I see the true Cockney spirit?

Tubing out of Highgate, on the Friday of the VE-Day anniversary weekend, I saw a fellow passenger perusing an official Tube Commemorative Journey Planner. Just the thing to organise my day, I thought. So, at Highgate, I asked for one at the ticket window. 'Sorry, mate,' said the obliging clerk after a long search through various drawers full of forms, 'we don't appear to 'ave any. Supplies of these kind of things don't reach us out 'ere. Ask in Central London.' As a provincial myself, I could sympathise, despite my mild astonishment at his feeling of being 'out here', where I considered was still the heart of the capital.

But his lack of planners got me my ten pound fine.

It happened the next morning, when I was rushing to catch an early Tube for Heathrow. It was just about six-thirty when I dashed into Highgate station. The ticket window was shut, so I just jumped on the first train. I needed to change from the Northern Line to the Piccadilly at King's Cross; what could be easier than to buy a ticket there – and pick up my Commemorative Journey Planner?

I went over to the window (mockingly marked 'Assistance') and, right enough, there was a pile of planners neatly stacked up. Waiting for the clerk, I stuffed three of them away. Then I asked for a ticket to Heathrow – and the interrogation began.

'Where have you come from?'

'Highgate.'

'Why didn't you get a ticket there?'

'Because the window was shut.'

'You should have used the machine.'

This was the moment I first realised that all Tube stations have automatic ticket machines and that you are expected to use them. It's the kind of convention that's well enough known to the regular user, but which is so easily missed by the outsider, despite all the warning notices. But I was trying to get to the airport to catch an early flight, and a long argument was the last thing I wanted. So the shortest answer seemed to be: 'I didn't have any change.'

'The machine gives change.'

'Look, I am a visitor. Are you going to give me a ticket?'

'It's an offence to travel without a ticket.'

'Look, I came up here to buy a ticket, are you going to give me one?'

'You should have a ticket before getting on the train. You're not allowed to travel without one. That's what the machines are for.'

And that's when I should have used the Scottish bank notes argument, because I discovered afterwards that was all I had – not the English pound coins or notes which, patriotically, is the only currency that the machines accept. But I just wanted away – though it wasn't going to be as easy as that.

'Where are you from?' was the next question.

'Glasgow. Will you give me a ticket?'

She wandered off to check with her atlas or to serve someone at the next window. She came back. 'There is a ten-pound penalty for travelling without a ticket.'

'You want me to pay ten pounds before you give me a ticket?'

'Yes.'

I stuffed fifteen pounds under the glass to cover the fine and the £3.30 for the ticket. She pushed the Scottish fiver back wordlessly – for the first time since we met last week – and started to write something out.

14

Halfway through this painful exercise, she started saying: 'If you want to appeal . . . '

'Aw, shut up,' I said. 'Just give me the ticket.'

'Don't you abuse me,' she said.

'Abuse you?' I said, 'all I want is a ticket, and you ask me where I'm from.'

'I need to know that so that I can make a decision.'

So there it was. She had discretion to make a judgment. If I had grovelled apologetically and answered 'I know, I know' to all of her harangues, I would have got off without a fine. But how can you play the game if you don't know the rules?

Anyway, I now had my Commemorative Journey Planner, a bit expensive at ten pounds, but useful nonetheless. It had a smart VE–Day logo, with little figures representing Britons from different walks of life, both then and now, decorating the front cover above the slogan 'You can't beat the Tube. Hitler didn't.' (I added that last sentence myself . . . it seemed to complete the message, somehow.)

Inside, there was an archive photo of two cheery Cockney Mrs Mopps serving tea and buns to even more cheerful Blitz dodgers, and a brief history of the Underground at war. 'While bombs rained down overhead, shelterers could rely on a steaming cup of tea, jam rolls and singalongs for comfort. Life underground was generally cheerful. Even Christmas was celebrated underground.'

This was exactly what I was looking for. This fitted entirely my preconceptions of the Dunkirk spirit that saw Britain sing its way through the war in the face of daunting odds and Goebbels' evil propaganda. And the Underground was right to strike that note. That weekend, it was what people most wanted to hear.

But official contemporary reports to which the leaflet referred made me wonder if this picture was so incomplete as to be highly misleading. For the official story made much grimmer reading.

During the Saturday night raid on 11 January 1941, Green Park, St Paul's, Baker St and Bank Stations were damaged, the latter station being severely damaged. There were fatal casualties at these stations, both to staff and to members of the public, but the details of the casualties are not yet available. It is practicable to use the stations for traffic as the damage does not interfere with the running of the trains, but it has been necessary to close Hyde Park Corner station owing to an unexploded bomb in the vicinity.

In fact, 56 people had been killed at Bank after a direct hit which caused the station to collapse and kept it closed for three months. The worst disaster during the war was three months earlier, on the Northern Line, where 68 people sheltering in Balham station were killed in October 1940. A bomb shattered the northbound station tunnel and ruptured nearby water mains and sewers, the contents of which rushed to fill the crater. But other wartime incidents were relatively minor, and the deep–level Tubes were undoubtedly safe places to be. None safer than the deepest below ground – the one I had just left that morning, the new Highgate station on the Northern line, which had been built but not opened when the war started. It was used solely as an air–raid shelter until 1945.

But, like all things in the modern world of the Tube, this eight–page leaflet meant business. It was a working document listing the extra services which were being provided to speed people to and from the celebrations. And promoting the cheap tickets which were available. Once again, the central role that the Tube plays in the everyday life of Londoners struck home.

I had to be in London for the party. Checking with *Time Out*, it appeared that the only local celebration that was in any way tied to a Tube station was at Ravenscourt Park, out west on the District Line. I determined to be there, before joining the mobs expected in Hyde Park.

So, just after two o'clock on the official Monday anniversary of VE–Day, I jumped on to the Piccadilly Line at Heathrow. The train lacked its usual quota of businessmen. Where before there was a throng milling about directionless, the concourse was deserted and the train half empty. Little Union Jacks were drawn in felt tip on the notice-board, which also announced that Hyde Park Corner station was shut due to overcrowding.

A curiously mixed–race family joined my carriage at Hatton Cross. As we drew into Hounslow Central, the sari-clad granny nudged the West Indian toddler in the push-chair, directing his attention to a cluster of tents in a field adjacent to the track.

16

'Is that part of the VE-Day celebrations?' I asked her.

'I don't think so,' she said. 'It's just May Day.'

Impulsively, I decided to abandon my plans to go straight to Ravenscourt Park and to follow the family instead. It would also give the crowds at Hyde Park station a chance to abate.

As I turned into Lampton Road, I realised that down here it was summer. The last time I had been in London, in March, it was still winter in Scotland, whereas the metropolis was enjoying spring, with the trees just beginning to bud. Now, the spring–like day I had left in Glasgow was transformed into hot summer. The trees were fully out, and the blossom and greenery overwhelmed me with that fresh smell of sun-induced growth.

Now I understood where all those barbecue sets advertised in the *Sunday Times* were sold. In Glasgow, we average one outdoor barbecue a summer. Here in London, the difference in climate is planetary.

The people are different, too. People surged along Lampton Road as if they were going to a football match. But most of them were black. This was just slightly less of a culture shock than the weather. In Glasgow, of course, we have immigrant communities, mainly Asian. And they have made an enormous contribution to the city. Not that there aren't problems or that racialism doesn't ever rear its head. But generally immigration is developing into integration.

Outside Lampton Park, a multi-coloured poster advertised the celebrations, and immediately stamped them as politically correct. This was 'A People's Peace and Unity Event' run by Hounslow Leisure Services. Not much doubt about where they were coming from. This must be one of the 'Looney Left' London Boroughs which had so exercised the tabloid press in the Eighties.

As an aid to peace and unity, the poster promised 'food from around the world', Bob Kerr's Whoppee Band, Irish Folk with Chanter, Malkit Singh and his Bhangra Band . . . and, topping the bill with Malkit, Jools Holland, who was then very big on British television.

I wandered past intense tennis players on the hard courts into the park and came across a notice announcing the start of the Sri Chinmoy mile route, a concept that combines fitness and world peace, I believe. The place was jumping. Hounslow Borough were

17

later to claim an aggregate attendance of 60,000 lovers of peace and unity. I wouldn't doubt it.

Certainly, sited between the neat flower beds, there were stalls selling food from around the world – including American hamburgers (how did they break the embargo?). And, on the hot grass, extended families and friends tucked into rice, pakora and other exotic fare. Haggis did not appear to be available.

There were clowns and face painters for the children. There was a Paul Robeson Theatre in a tent where what looked like school choirs performed without having the faintest idea which team he played for. Could one of these choirs have been the advertised 'thirty-strong gospel choir, surprisingly from Croydon'! There were Chinese lantern-making stands, drum workshops, bucking broncos, a ski simulator.

There was also alleged to be a 'children's striker' – but, not knowing what I was looking for, I never found it, him or her. Maybe it was an industrial relations workshop.

Music from reggae to pop and jazz and what I was told was bhangra blared out from the radio roadshow. Bhangra, the helpful borough employee told me, was Pakistani pop music.

I recalled the poster at the gate, 'Malkit Singh's Bhangra Band' it had read. 'Not if it's being played by someone called Singh, surely?' I asked diffidently in the face of such obviously overwhelming ethnic expertise.

'Oh well, maybe it's Indian, then. It's got lots of drums, anyway.'

I saw an insurance company desperately trying to compile a database by raffling a magnum of champagne. In the Youth Tent, DJ Mo presented a 'House against Hate' disco. I heard that, and was not tempted to investigate.

But, despite an exhaustive search, I missed entirely the Tabularasa and Hounslow Ethnic Monitoring Anti-Racism Marquee. Enquiries to discover what went on there elicited very little information. Tabularasa sponsored the marquee. Who they were, what they did, nobody knew. But, more intriguingly, what went on inside the Tabularasa and Hounslow Ethnic Monitoring Anti-Racism Marquee? Who was being monitored? And what happened to them if the results were negative – or, worse, positive? I was never told.

Neither did I see a single Union Jack. I heard the same complaint from a woman to her husband as they ushered their three children home.

'Not a mention of VE-Day,' she said resentfully.

I broke into her conversation, 'It's funny. I noticed that too. Why do you think it is?'

'It's that Hounslow Council,' she said. 'They just look after the minorities.'

Back on the Tube, I planned my journey to Ravenscourt Park. I would take the Piccadilly Line to Hammersmith and come back one stop on the District Line. As the train pulled in, I noticed that it had crossed Union Jacks on the front in recognition of the day.

The station at Ravenscourt Park is tucked discreetly up a side street just off King Street, Hammersmith. The nearest entrance to the park itself is equally well disguised. An unkempt, narrow path between back gardens and the railway viaduct was so discouraging that I had to be reassured by asking a couple walking the other way if I was on the right road.

'You can't miss it' turned out for once to be true because, a hundred yards on, there it was. A much grottier affair, this one. There was a permanent sign indicating that the park was in Hammersmith and Fulham. But there were no posters advertising the event, though thousands had been printed as commemoratives. The one the council sent me later advertised a beacon lighting ceremony for the Saturday night, which anticipated the Queen's official performance by some two days!

The posters also advised that there would be a limit on numbers 'permitted entry into the parks'. For safety reasons, presumably. They needn't have worried. Judging by the numbers I saw, the council tax payers of Hammersmith and Fulham were highly safety conscious.

Thin music leaked from a distorting PA system. I wandered over to a cluster of deserted seats in front of a bare stage. On it, gyrating in the most politically incorrect way, was a teenage girl. A half-deflated bouncy castle attracted a short queue of double parents and children. A pink bus from the borough council almost attracted interest.

This was much more like the British fairs that I was used to. There were a series of tired, half-empty fairground rides. Even the weather was cooler. I could see plenty of this at home, so I decided to head for Hyde Park. In terms of putting on a successful event the comrades from Hounslow had won hands down. But a competition is something that they probably wouldn't enter.

Back on the train again, I picked up a discarded newspaper. It was the previous day's *Welt am Sonntag* – 'The Sunday Paper for Germany' was how I translated its front page motto. German visitors making their way to London today? Very interesting. Interesting, too, that London's VE-Day celebration made only a small paragraph and a picture of the Queen Mother on page three.

Although the train all the way in was quiet, Hyde Park Corner station was still closed. So I got off one stop early at Knightsbridge. Harrods was shut.

There seemed to be more people walking from the park than to it. But they were taking VE-Day seriously. Packed taxis drove by with Union Jacks flying from their radio masts. There were Union Jack balloons, Union Jack hats and Union Jack tee–shirts. And, of course, flags to wave.

I wandered into the park just as the Household Cavalry was walking out. Their pomp and pageantry was somewhat betrayed by the presence of two mounted policemen leading them across the road. The horse box marked 'Horses in Transit' which followed them looked less than military, too.

The anniversary of VE-Day, according to the *Daily Telegraph*, saw 'events to rival the Coronation'. Fifty heads of state arrived in London and were deprived of the use of their official cars for transferring from Buckingham Palace to Hyde Park. They were bussed instead because of the security headache which individual arrivals would have caused. A wonderful egalitarian touch, on this most democratic of days.

In the park, they sat in a special 500-seater 'Royal' box, flanked by two 5,000-seater stands for slightly lesser VIPs. Clearly, one didn't want to take egalitarianism too far.

But the public were to be there in force. Eight hundred thousand of us turned out. And fully prepared, at that. The tabloids fully briefed their readers on the historic last battles that had led to Germany's unconditional surrender. Little maps with converging arrows showed how the Reich had been squeezed to death between the Russians (red arrows) on the one hand and the British and Americans (blue arrows) on the other. Just down the pages from these historical perspectives, similar graphics showed how to obtain the best views of the celebrations. You could pick a vantage point to see the heads of state (red arrows) or the fireworks (blue arrows). At either site you would be squeezed to death.

Over the three days of the festivities, 20,000 entertainers performed alongside Vera Lynn, poor soul. At the Albert Hall, the National Symphony Orchestra performed a programme of wartime favourites interspersed with grainy Pathe newsreel. The Queen, the Queen Mother and Princess Margaret appeared on the balcony of Buckingham Palace to re-enact the scene that they had performed there in 1945. This time it was in colour. Cliff Richard completed his transformation from rebel pop star to Knight Bachelor by leading the masses in The Mall as they sang *Congratulations*. Nobody cared that it was the song that had NOT won the Eurovision Song Contest. There was a Spitfire, a Hurricane, a Hawk trainer and a Euro–fighter scattered throughout the 60-acre site. This was the last chance to see a barrage balloon as, immediately after the event, the RAF's balloon squadron was disbanded.

I took that chance, but, apart from the balloon, which did trigger childhood memories, I saw very little. The overcrowding, and my detour to Hounslow, had meant that I had arrived at Hyde Park much later than I had planned. As I walked in through the Albert Gate, the flag seller was still doing good business. 'Fly your flags. Any more now, your flags.' But he was selling to people leaving the park, not those going in. As I moved in, his cries were overwhelmed by those of the amplified official announcer, instructing vendors to close their stalls. 'We do not want you selling at this time.' The afternoon party was over and the park had to be cleared to prepare for the evening bash which was to begin at eight o'clock.

I passed by a dissembling band of young girls and boys, many of whom were romantically involved with each other. It was their uniforms that stood out. They were green, white and gold – the Irish national colours. Even with the progress of the peace process in Northern Ireland, this was surely going a bit too far – or was it simply naïve? The band's name, Alconbury, was on every player's back. When I approached, I could hear that they all had American accents.

21

'What part of the States are you from?' I asked one.

'I'm from Massachusetts, and she's from Illinois.'

'No, I mean Alconbury.'

'That's near Cambridge.'

'So, the school is in Massachusetts?' I said to impress her with my knowledge of American geography.

'No, I mean Cambridge, England. Our dads are in the American air force.'

I was determined to see something of the displays, but the central area of the park was cordoned off with a high wire-mesh perimeter fence. Through it, I could see the Hawk trainer and the Euro-fighter. The signs on the latter were in English and German, 'Danger' and 'Achtung' painted side by side. A strange irony or a hopeful sign of the progress made in the last 50 years?

I wandered round the fence on my way to Hyde Park Corner station, passing a few pot smokers, undisturbed by the police, and a Dog Toby with a red, white and blue ruff. Its owner typified the mood of the crowd. He was there in both party and patriotic mood. He had come here to take part in history and he was enjoying it thoroughly.

I walked with the crowds past the still-congested station up to Piccadilly. In the enormous queue for the Hard Rock café were scores of men in British service uniforms of all branches and eras. It looked like a queue for the catering lorry on a film set. Across the road on the palings of Green Park – iron railings that would have been sawn off and carried away for the war effort in 1940 – were the garish goods of the stallholders. Real tourist traps these, they were selling lurid paintings of London, brass works, mock leather bags.

I crossed over to buy a souvenir of the day. But it was all so ghastly. I thought about some foreign stamps – from the Empire, say. But they would just lie in a drawer beside my boyhood collection and never be seen.

The second-hand bookstall looked the most promising. Without any effort I found a Penguin edition of Churchill's *My Early Life*. Originally priced at six shillings, it was now marked in pencil at £1.50. Ideal – and, given the rate of inflation, a lot cheaper than when it first went on sale. What a happy coincidence to find it so easily.

I thumbed through it. It fell open at Page 261 where Louis Botha, Prime Minister of the Transvaal, is in London in 1906 and is warning Churchill against the Germans. 'Do not trust those people. They mean mischief.' For all of us, thankfully, it was a warning that Churchill, all of his life, never forgot.

Vera Lynn reverberated throughout Green Park station, interrupted only by an announcement that Hyde Park Corner station was still 'closed for exit due to a very large number of people trying to get into a very small station'. That wry Cockney humour again!

That was when the implications of the day really got through to me. I looked around at the ordinary Londoners sitting beside me. Men and women of all ages, families. Most of them clearly were fairly poor, working-class people. I could see their predecessors 50 years ago travelling the same Tube – to work, to war, to do their bit. They just seemed so English. It was through people like this that England had been able to build an Empire, to rule three-quarters of the world and, in their finest hour, to stand against barbaric dictatorship and for humanity. They were right to celebrate.

I had seen the same kind of attitude from afar during and after the Falklands War – from the indignation of the House of Commons and the jingoism after each victory to the vulgarity of the Thatcher victory parade. But that was a parody, a circus for the people. Or, rather, let's face it, for one person – the Iron Lady herself.

This was different. This was a reminder that England had been truly heroic in 1940. I say England, because I saw very distinct differences with Scotland. Certainly the Falklands War had been treated with great suspicion in Scotland, and rightly. But even the VE-Day celebrations were lower key up there. For one thing, it wasn't even a public holiday. My office worked on the official VE Monday. There were few of the publicly or privately organised events that took place throughout England.

The Scots had been very happy to tag along around the Empire, and in many cases to do very well. We had played our full part in the war. But we wouldn't have initiated either. That was for big nations to do. And Scotland is a small nation.

I was due to stay with a friend in Putney that night, but I had to get off the Tube at Piccadilly – just to be able to say that I had been there that day. But very little was happening. Eros in its new position was boarded up. The crowds were thin. The only thing to interest them was Judith Chalmers doing a piece to camera for some independent producer's outside broadcast. It probably wasn't even live.

I began to retrace my steps on the Piccadilly Line, changing at Barons Court for Putney Bridge. Walking from the station to the bridge, I passed an old folk's home smothered in bunting. Through the open french window, I could see an old soldier in a wheelchair with his army beret on, watching the coverage from Hyde Park on the telly.

The bells of St Mary's, Putney, pealed out a victory salute as I crossed the bridge that took over 150 years to build. It was first proposed in 1571, but vehement opposition from the Company of Watermen, who fought any challenge to their monopoly of transport, delayed its construction until 1729. It was such dogged and blind resistance in the face of the inevitable that defeated Hitler.

I stopped to take a photo of the church, with its flag of St George. A teenage girl jumped in front of the camera grinning. I saw her Munich University sweat shirt. 'You must be German,' I shouted after her, but her reply was lost in the wind.

I walked along the tree-lined suburban streets of terraced houses. I passed a couple of street parties that were still going on under flags stretched across the road. I was going to stop for a chat. But these were celebrations for neighbours and friends and I didn't want to intrude.

I went to my friend's for something to eat, put my feet up and watched the Hyde Park fireworks on the telly. A different kind of tube, performing the same kind of unifying role which the Underground had done so magnificently for London for so many years.

CHAPTER TWO

CRICKET AT COCKFOSTERS

One day I did something I'd been tempted to do for years. I got on the tube at Heathrow and stayed on all the way to Cockfosters.

I had been flying down to London for years on business, catching the breathless Tube into town and dashing back to the airport at the end of a day of turgid meetings. What else do you do on the Tube but sit and stare out of the windows, whether you are underground or not? The names of the stations I passed began to fascinate me. Had there been a medieval lord at Boston Manor? Why Barons Court and Earl's Court? What would I find if I took the wrong train and ended up in Rayners Lane? And were there actually people who could live in a place called Cockfosters and keep a straight face?

For me, required to repeat the one journey back and forward, month after month, the Tube created a kind of longing to break out of the strictures of my routine. I would look at the map fascinated, studying the station names and trying to capture some idea of the places they represented. The attractive mult-coloured scheme added to the romance and offered the prospect of exploration and discovery. It was a map of territory unknown to me, of places which promised fun, excitement, novelty and interest. And yet, it was comfortably confined and reassuringly limited. I had to find out what was out there.

My instinct was just to go and do it one day. Get on the Tube at Piccadilly and head for Uxbridge rather than the airport. But business schedules command. It would mean missing a 'plane, postponing a meeting, having to find a hotel and staying over. I realised that I couldn't just do it on impulse. The journey had to be an end in itself if I were to capture anything other than the frustration of a commuter. So I planned a special trip. And I discussed it with friends and colleagues, none of whom could get the least excited about it. But talking about it built up my own expectations and I saw the possibilities of exploring London, not in the conventional way, but by using the Underground network as my guide. I knew that Henry Beck's famous map of the system – he was paid five guineas in 1933 for creating it – bore little relation to geography. But that didn't matter to me, as I didn't *know* the geography of London. It would add to the fun of finding out, while the inflexibility that it imposed would be a fine structure for the journey. I wouldn't have to wander about trying to figure out where to go next, I'd just go back to the station and get on the next train. So, when Raine, my secretary, ran me to Glasgow airport, I really was setting out on an adventure.

'See and not get mugged,' was her cheery, waving farewell as she dropped me off.

Was this how Paul Theroux was seen off in Massachusetts as he caught the train for Patagonia? Was it some such concern that caused Mrs Bryson to keep the car and make Bill see Glasgow by taxi? Marco Polo's P.A. must have been pretty apprehensive, too. But did she let it show? If she was worried, she needn't have been because, as we now know, the brave Italian never went near China.

But Raine's remark – not entirely sarcastic – made me feel even more like a real traveller setting off into the dangerous unknown. Not that I needed to get into that mood. That *was* how I felt. This was an adventure I was looking forward to as much as any. London had held a magic for me since I had dropped the house keys down a drain in Islington.

That was 1954. I was 14 and suffering from boarding school. But I got a lucky break. Pope Pius XII, the pope of my childhood and therefore *the* Pope, just as George VI was *the* King and Foxhunter was *the* Olympic gold-medallist, helped me out. (In case you don't remember Foxhunter, I'd better explain. Britain had a disastrous 1952 Olympics. Our only gold medal winner was Colonel Harry Llewellyn in the show jumping. Foxhunter carried him to victory). The school which held me was run by a religious order, and the Pope announced the beatification of its founder, the Venerable Marcellin Champagnat. Naturally, as many as possible of the little souls that his followers were saving had to be present at the ceremony. So a trip to Rome was organised, and I was selected to travel. Not on grounds of merit, I should add. My parents could afford to let me go, that was all.

We broke the journey in London at the provincial headquarters of the order, in Islington. As we stood outside the house waiting for a bus to take us on a tour of the city, some teacher was daft enough to hand me the keys of the place for safe-keeping. Why, I do not know. Because I was not one of those generally entrusted with such things. I was a kind of average pupil who never got the good jobs of taking messages from one classroom to another, or handing out the milk, or cleaning the blackboard. But I used to do that anyway after the teacher had left, just for the fun of getting covered in chalk.

Anyway, there I was standing on the pavement with my Dexter firmly buckled over my blazer, my cap on my head, throwing this huge bunch of keys up and down. Of course, I dropped them and, of course, they fell down a drain.

So, while the rest went off to see the sights of London, I had to hang around the drain and wait for the cleansing department to turn up to try to find them. I am now not sure whether this was a punishment or simply that someone had to wait for help. No, I'm sure it was a punishment.

But the hanging around gave me time to think. It was then that I first experienced the feeling of unreality that foreign travel produces. 'I'm in London . . . London . . . LONDON' I kept repeating, until the word lost its meaning. Because I couldn't quite grasp the reality of being somewhere else at the same time when, back home, people were carrying on their normal routine. Whether it was the longing for the mundane routine of family life that boarding school had produced, and of which I day-dreamed every single day of my six years' incarceration, I don't know. But London as an actual place in an actual time was no more real than AD 43 or 1066 or 1606. Despite the fact that I was standing in it.

Today that feeling is still one of the greatest thrills I find travelling, especially across time zones. I also love the feeling that Bombay or Dar-es-Salaam has been opened up simply for your benefit and that, as your 'plane is taxi-ing out for take-off, they're putting the whole thing away, only to be ready to bring it out again in time for your next visit.

Anyway, back in 1954, I continued to stand there – I'd been warned under pain of death not to move – trying to orientate myself. I was always unconvinced by the look of bewilderment shown by each of Dr Who's new female helpers as she emerged for the first time from the *Tardis* to start a new adventure. Over-acting at its most primitive, I used to think. But, 25 years before *Dr Who*, that's exactly how I felt. Only I wasn't acting at all.

I was quite enjoying myself.

Then a big, maroon, Corporation sucker truck came round the corner. That was how I knew I was in Islington. It said so on the side of the vehicle. Two men jumped down. I was unused to dealing with any adults other than teachers, and expected a row for wasting their time. But they weren't bothered. They just lifted the drain cover with a couple of hooks, sucked up all the mud and there were the keys, lying on a ledge about four feet down. I was amazed to see them again.

But then, as I remember it, came the problem of what to do with me. I couldn't catch up with the tour, and I couldn't be left behind. There was one teacher left, and he had to go to the Italian Embassy to fix some boy's passport. I had to go, too. It wasn't a sightseeing tour. But he did his best, pointing things out as we went along, none of which I can remember. He took me on a London bus with appropriate ceremony, making sure that it was moving before we jumped on the platform. And he took me on the Tube – no-one else got to do that.

Maybe it was that experience – a tantalising, unfulfilled taster of London – which had led me to this present exploration? At any rate, here I was at Heathrow, ready to start.

Incidentally, Blessed Marcellin Champagnat still waits on the threshold of sainthood. He was pursuing his holy work just after the French Revolution but it wasn't until 1954 that he took the penultimate step, and he's been on it ever since. Not that 40-odd years is long in the life of the Church. One of Scotland's very few saints, the Jesuit, St John Ogilvie, who was martyred at Glasgow Cross in 1615, was not beatified until 1929 and not canonised until 1976. And another, the internationally known theologian, John Duns Scotus, took from the 13th century to the late 20th to be recognised as a saint.

Terminal One is normally a place you leave as fast as possible. You've got an appointment in London. You're generally tight for time. So you rush down for Tube or taxi. But I was on my holidays. I felt a bit sick, too – a combination of a bumpy descent and the sight of the unaccompanied minor beside me trying to be sick into a bag. So I took my time to leave the airport, wandering into the self-service restaurant for a plate of soup – something you would never do if you were down on business.

As I wandered into the airport restaurant, I reflected on what an imposition in-flight children are on the rest of the flying public and how this interminable problem could be tackled. I once met a sheikh in Dubai who valued his hunting birds so highly that he had a Boeing 707 specially kitted out for them to fly separately but in comfort as he journeyed with them around the Middle East. I would insist that British Airways made the same arrangement for children under 15. I know it's wrong to complain about children. And I know that I shouldn't be grumpy, bad-tempered and a touch intolerant. But I find nothing worse on boarding a 'plane than to find that I'm stuck behind a father, mother, moaning toddler and hysterical baby. This is especially galling if I have been fortunate enough to find myself, through some benign computer error, upgraded to Business Class. So, for a start, I'd confine kids to Economy. But, I suspect that so many people feel like me that they would gladly pay a surcharge for a 'no children' flight. 'No other people's children', that is. My granddaughter, even at only 15 months old, is a model traveller.

The grass at Heathrow Airport is kept eight inches high, because at that height none of the ten types of birds that use the airport can see predators coming. So they avoid settling. In Sydney, the grass has to be tall enough to hide an emu, I guess.

Heathrow was the place where Princess Elizabeth, as the new Queen, first set foot on British soil, flying in from Kenya where she had been when her father died. This fact is commemorated in the coat of arms of the local borough, Hillingdon. Only Prestwick Airport can claim a greater honour. It was the only place in Britain where that other monarch, Elvis, was ever seen – when he was alive, that is.

On the site of the airport – we're back to Heathrow now – the round huts and temple of an Iron Age village dating from 500 BC were discovered in 1944. What should we call our age? Aluminium? Plastic? Virtual?

Heathrow is not just one of the world's busiest airports, it's a generator of extraordinary statistics. The airport covers 4.6 square miles and, for every inch and a half of snow that falls, 74,000 tonnes have to be removed just to keep the 'planes flying. Over 50,000 people are employed there, doing everything from talking in the 550 aircraft that land every day to serving the 26,000 cups of tea or the 6,500 pints of beer that are drunk day in, day out. There's even one guy waiting 360 days of the year to remove the snow.

The revenues from the airport's landing and other charges are almost matched by the scale of its retailing operations, which account for £200 million per year. The retail space at the airport is greater than many town centres. And classier. But there was no good greetings card shop, a lack that caused me no end of grief. I'll come to that.

In practical terms, this means Heathrow's sales of perfume account for nine per cent of the whole British market. The books sold at the airport amount to about four per cent of all those sold in Britain. Heathrow sells 350 bottles of Scotch, 20 bottles of champagne and 40 lipsticks every hour. The Swatch shop measures only 312 square feet but manages to sell 78,000 watches a year. No one can count the amount of litter dropped in the four terminals, but one tonne of the stuff is collected from the airfield – I mean the bird-deterring grass and the runways – every day.

From the days of the Royal Flying Corps during World War I, this part of Middlesex has always been associated with flying. But it was not until 1946 that the first passenger flight left from Heathrow. On New Year's Day, a converted Lancaster bomber of British South American Airways left for Buenos Aires via Lisbon. It carried ten passengers. Today, 50 million people fly from Heathrow to over 220 destinations on a choice of 90 airlines.

I thought that I had seen the world's largest collection of taxis, at Delhi airport. But evidently Heathrow's taxi gathering park, with 500 cabs, runs it close. Every driver waits between two and three hours to get a fare. No wonder they're always in a foul mood. Years ago, I made the mistake of asking one to take me to Osterley. 'Nothing but filth all day,' he muttered. Then he threw me into a taxi just coming in the main gate and went back to try to retrieve his place in the queue for a more remunerative journey. To him I was probably just part of the one tonne of litter collected every day.

One final historical note relating to what is now part of the airport site: in 1784, near the Three Magpies Inn on the Bath Road, a British army officer, Major General William Roy, measured a baseline five and a quarter miles from Hounslow Heath to Hampton Hill. From that line grew the Ordnance Survey and all those fascinating maps with their symbols for pubs, churches and Red Indian villages which disappointingly turn out to be camp sites.

After finishing my soup and jettisoning the rubbish in a bin in the best American fast food tradition, I was off down to the Tube past a sign advertising free hotel reservations. Was that a selling point? I have never known anyone to charge for a hotel reservation. I wandered up to the ticket window and got served right away. It was March and the tourist season hadn't begun. I was to learn that, at the height of the summer, the queue for the windows could be 30 or 40 non-English-speaking people long and that it was essential to carry change to feed the automatic ticket machines. It took me months to discover that the little London Transport Information booth, one floor down from the shuttle gate, opposite the luggage carousels, also sells tickets. And you generally get served right away. A day ticket for that day and one for the next as well, was what I asked for and what I got. 'How long will it take me to get to Cockfosters?' I asked the ticket clerk, more to see whether she knew than because it really mattered. 'About an hour and a half,' was the answer that proved accurate.

Then, with the platform's digital clock showing 13.13, it was on to the train. I squeezed on beside the Brazilian youth football team that had just lost to Scotland. Excited young Portuguese voices chanting 'London', 'Piccadilly'. How much will that lot be worth in three or four years' time? Maybe not too much if they lost to Scotland! The driver discourages the runners trying to board as the doors shut. 'Get the next train along behind.' It could be the Tube's motto.

A child was asking her father, 'Is the Red Sea red?' I thought at first it was a figure of speech, like 'Is Wogan Irish?', and, verbally advanced for her 11 years, she was demonstrating her mastery of irony. But it seemed a genuine quest for information. I wanted to tell her the explanation that I had read, that it comes from a misreading of 'reed' in an early translation. But that can't be right, can it? Because it wouldn't then be 'Red' in other languages, unless English had been the language of the first translation. But is it 'Mer Rouge' in French? I'd better check that. Then the child showed her total confusion by speculating how she would just lie on her back and float in the Red Sea. Her older brother tried to interrupt with all the knowledge of his 13 years, but their mother kindly shushed him quiet. She was enjoying hearing her daughter talk and the animation in her eyes.

Don't make the mistake of getting off at Hatton Cross. You're still in the airport there, only it's the servants' entrance.

Near Northfields, I saw a workman with a measuring tape and plan, sizing up a broken garage door. That feeling of travelling outside reality, outside the mundane, everyday tasks that engaged other people, swept over me again. The family got up to leave. As they waited for the doors to open, the boy prodded his sister on the arm. 'It's the Dead Sea,' he said. 'That's what I said,' she shouted as she jumped on to the platform.

Then the driver had trouble with his speaker system. He had been using this to give the mandatory warning about the gap as the doors opened at every station. So ingrained in London culture is this phrase that the new Wonderbra ad was that summer carrying 'Mind the Gap' as its tag line. This, of course, is a wonderfully clever idea, reminding passengers of the product by the announcement at every station. And it is not an unpleasant thing to be reminded about.

Just before South Ealing the driver forgot to cradle his phone. Maybe he was thinking about the Wonderbra. After his nasal 'Mind the Gap', we could hear someone broadcasting to him. If I'd heard that on a 'plane, I would have been totally unnerved, reading disaster into the words I could only partially hear. But if I'd been shaking around like this in a 'plane, I would have thought we were going to crash. It is amazing how we have different expectations of stability on different forms of transport. Most people come to 'planes after having experienced buses and trains. And 'planes are much more stable. So any turbulence puts people on the edges of their seats. My own children had travelled, perfectly behaved, with us on 'planes many times. But the two girls had never been on a train until the younger one was five. As the train pulled out, it gave the usual sort of shudder as the carriages bumped into each other before settling down into its rhythm of motion. Familiar to us, but the girls were terrified. 'Planes had never been as bumpy as this.

On the left on the way into Turnham Green, there is a church surrounded by grass which is criss-crossed with paths. A planner once told me that, in laying out large housing schemes around areas of open space, he would leave the ground bare and see where people wear their own paths. Then he would grass and pave the appropriate areas. 'We've experimented with that for three years. That's why we just concrete everything from the start!' he concluded. He was right. No one was using these paths. People were walking everywhere but the paths.

At South Kensington, snatches of Ravel's *Bolero* blew through the doors, and a man with the only American red-and-black checked hunting hat I'd seen outside a cartoon came with them. Another man in a smart business suit and short hair had come on with a sheaf of music, which he read like a novel. At Piccadilly Circus, he recognised a passenger who was getting off, and they exchanged friendly greetings. Was this a unique Tube moment? I certainly never saw anyone recognise anyone else in all of the rest of my journeys.

The train all but emptied at Piccadilly Circus. In my carriage, there was only me and the music reader left. But the spaces were soon filled by other travellers with their own destinations and appointments to the east.

A young German or Norwegian boy came on with his school group, sat opposite me and said hello. I was shocked. Because it seemed a breach of Underground protocol to speak to strangers.

We came overground just before Arnos Grove. My first view was of two multi-storeys, but that was misleading as there were more signs of affluence here than at the western end of the line. The 1930s houses were further back than those in the west, the gardens longer and the railway higher above them. There was a bowling green instead of a crazy golf course. But some developer had been cynical enough to build new houses as close to the track as those at Heathrow. And was that a real golf course I saw through the trees?

I heard the train's whistle. Until then, I hadn't known that Tube trains had whistles.

Cockfosters at last. As I climbed the station stairs, I had that warm feeling of achievement that you are supposed to experience at the end of any journey. Journeys are good. But it is great to arrive. It means you can start another journey. This was the place on the Underground that I had wanted to reach. I was eager to see what was here. But these thoughts made me laugh. This was a Tube station, a commuter suburb, not even a town. I shouldn't be excited about this.

But I was. And not just because I had found out the derivation of the name of the place. It is evidently of French origin, dating back to the Norman Conquest when William parcelled out this particular part of England to one of his knights, Baron de Mandeville. It was then a part of Enfield Chase (or forest) and much used by the bold Norman for hunting. 'Fosters' is a corruption of 'forestiere' or forester. Of that the authorities are agreed. There is an argument over the 'cock'. Some say it comes from 'bicoque', a collection of huts where the foresters lived. Others argue it refers to the hut of the 'coq de forestieres', the head forester. So, I suppose we could think of Cockfosters as the Village of the Foresters.

Four centuries passed and nothing much happened. Correction, nothing happened. Then came the War of the Roses, and still nothing happened to put Cockfosters on the map. There was a battle where Warwick the Kingmaker was slain. But that was just up the road, at Barnet.

Another century or two passed by and a legend sprung up. Dick Turpin is said to have holed up locally. I know that's not much of a legend, but, at that time, Cockfosters wasn't much of a place. However, it wasn't the only time that this most famous of highwaymen was going to crop up on my journey round the Underground.

Cockfosters was so insignificant that, even by 1833, its name appeared on no map. Throughout the nineteenth century it was only the church that brought the village to wider attention.

Until the arrival of the Tube. That changed it – rudely and permanently. Its advent was, however, by no means universally deplored. The local chronicler, writing in the parish magazine, greeted it thus:

Cockfosters! An odd name and surely a very pretty one,

suggestive of a pleasant and peaceful place . . . A few years back and our hamlet was unknown to London at large . . . Now a great change is upon us . . . little Cockfosters, with its 'decent church that topp'd the neighbouring hill', its comely inn, its green cricket field and its gracious pastures, is shaken from its smiling seclusion . . . THE TUBE IS COMING. The motor–shovel is coughing valiantly, and making mighty incisions into the meadows. Look over the five-barred gate next to the boys' school, or through the hedge of what used to enclose the polo ground, and behold the changing of a fair natural face. Oh, we are making no lament! Such things must be . . . The changes upon us and upon our village have at any rate earned us already a distinction which many places, long populous and prominent, have never yet achieved. We have been honoured by a poet in Punch . . .

To the tune of Cock Robin:
> *'Who said "Cockfosters"?'*
> *'I' said the Underground,*
> *'I'll shovel asunder ground,*
> *I said "Cockfosters".'*

And so on, for five excruciating verses.

But, despite these sanguine thoughts, the coming of the Underground was disruptive. The *Palmers Green and Southgate Gazette* reported in January 1932 that 'down in the valley, towards Southgate, giant metal arms of grabs and scoops have excavated clay and made foundations for the 400-foot viaduct that will span the dip over which the line will pass. All day you can hear the rumble of small trolleys and hammering on the supports and stays while, perched high on the brickwork, nimble bricklayers place in position the bricks of this graceful extension.' All this activity brought with it the usual complaints of nuisance, especially by heavy lorries. They ran every night, carrying supplies and waste material along quiet suburban roads, and found rat runs along the country lanes.

McAlpine and Co. had to pay threepence a mile compensation for the damage to the roads that their trucks caused. And, of course, there were complaints about the visual impact of the buildings, electrical sub-stations coming in for particular criticism. Don't they always?

The cost from Hounslow West to Cockfosters, the whole length of the line in 1933, was 1/– (5p). Is it cheaper today at £3.30? Using the Mars Bar Index, a measure devised by a whimsical financial journalist to measure the value of goods and services by the number of those sweets that could be swapped for them in the different years, the answer is 'probably'.

But for the writer, the visitor, what an appropriate first sight greets you at Cockfosters. Directly opposite the station is Cockfosters Cricket Club. What an English scene I could paint here. Bat on ball, willow on leather, flannelled villagers, warm summer evenings, and pints of the warm beer about which John Major, a cricket fan, eulogises.

And, beyond that, an English churchyard. Was this a Stoke Poges? It didn't look very old. In fact it was built in 1839. The church was brick, not stone. But they use a lot of brick in England. It was shut. I had better wander through the churchyard and check the dates. The graves were not very old. Francis Bevan, with his honours, JP DL, caught my eye. Not much good to you on a tombstone. Not much good to you before that either.

There seemed to be a lot of these Bevans. Among the more interesting was Anthony Bevan, born 1859, who was Lord Almoner and Professor of Arabic at Cambridge University before he died in 1933. He must have known T.E. Lawrence.

The Bevan boys gave me the key to the founder of the church, Francis's father, Robert Cooper Lee Bevan. He came from a South Wales family of Quakers who, with their relatives and business partners, the Barclays, founded a little firm called Barclay, Tritton and Bevan, which expanded its name along with its trade and became Barclay, Bevan, Tritton, Ransom, Bouverie and Co. A primitive marketing ploy to emphasise respectability and stability? Or simply the ego of the founding partners? Even later, when it had expanded sufficiently to have the confidence to rely on a shorter name, it became Barclay's, the bank. So Robert could well afford to build the odd church or two. He probably thought that it was a good investment.

I wandered up Cockfosters Road. I was in the borough of Enfield.

This was a rich place if the shops were anything to go by. And shops were all there appeared to be. There was the Wrought Iron Shop, which was exclusively devoted to selling the whole range of useless, expensive items for the fireplace. And indoor gnomes. The outdoor ones had been on sale further down the street in the same shop as the 'Nappy Family' drying rack. There were plenty of restaurants, Italian, Indian, Chinese and a World of Kosher. There was a bathing costume made of the same material as the shower curtains it was displayed against. There was Broadfield's Land Rover franchise and a mock-Dickensian solicitors' office. There were boutiques, including LA Connection. Surely there wasn't the remotest connection between LA and Cockfosters?

But I had business to do. I had to buy a birthday card for my daughter. 'There's a good card shop at the airport,' the girls at the office had promised me.

'No there is not,' I phoned them from the concourse half an hour later. 'You didn't just say that in case I sent you out to buy one for me?' I enquired tentatively, horrified at the image that they had of me as a parent.

'Well, last week you sent me out for a lawnmower blade. And the week before Gillian spent two hours trailing round looking for something for your sensitive teeth. And the week before that . . .'

'But none of those were personal gifts,' I protested.

'We weren't taking any chances.'

There wasn't a card shop at Heathrow, either. So here I was having to remember to buy my daughter a birthday card on my holiday. But now it could double as a souvenir from Cockfosters.

The shop did have cards, but not a great selection. There seemed to be more emphasis on artists' materials. Was this what they did at nights here, paint pictures? But I would have to get one here. I took my selection to the owner and handed over a Clydesdale Bank ten pound note. A great debate followed.

'Oh,' said the next customer queuing up at the till behind me waiting to pay for her selection of paints and brushes, 'is that Scottish? I've never seen one like that.'

'Mrs, I'm in enough trouble already,' I joked, grinning reassuringly at the shopkeeper's daughter who had come out of the back-shop to help.

'Scottish is all right. It's Irish you can't take,' the artist wittered on to the suspicious shopkeeper.

'Look, here's my boarding pass. I just flew down this morning.'

For some reason that swung it and I got out with my card. I've had less trouble in Spain.

Back on the train, I walked over a copy of that morning's *Times*. Free newspapers, just like British Airways. I was going back, retracing my journey, wanting to pick up those stations whose names caught my fancy.

First stop, Arnos Grove. Coming up the stairs, I nearly bumped into four youths, four dogs and four cans of lager. A little exhibition in the station told me the history of the place. 'Arnos Grove station was called after a street of the same name. The name itself dates back to the 14th century and is associated with the family of Margery Arnold. It is recorded as Arnoldes Grove in 1551.'

There is a wide variety of architectural styles on the Piccadilly Line. The ones at this station, at nearby Southgate and at Sudbury Town in the west are the most important. Built by Charles Holden, they are now listed buildings. Arnos Grove station was the first to have the circular or drum-type booking hall best known in Piccadilly Circus. As far as I could see at Arnos Grove there is just a row of shops – and less interesting ones than Cockfosters, at that. Except for the Keflourisos F.C. Club – 'Members Only'. What went on in there? Greek football?

Of course, I had missed the architecturally-interesting station at Southgate. So back I went. Sitting in front of me was a British Airways stewardess in uniform with her distinctive suitcase on trolley. Why live so far away from Heathrow? Or is this the real value of the Tube, linking distant places so effortlessly?

This time I noticed that, although the line was on the surface, Southgate station itself was underground in a short tunnel. At first, this more costly design seemed a bit daft, with passengers having to use the stairs to get to and from the trains. But it emphasises how no expense was spared to get the station architecturally and aesthetically right, because this design gave a much more spacious station which nevertheless did not over-dominate its surroundings. That effort was in vain because a large shopping centre, far less sympathetic, has been allowed to grow up around it. There was a much better card shop here. Like the one at Cockfosters, this also had arty–farty stuff. And knitting wool for making woollen dolls – which were displayed in the window but oddly enough were not for sale. A pity, as I now knew I needed a birthday present, too.

Then I began to make my way back to town. Finsbury Park is a clean, modern station. On the way out there is a T-junction, one way being Out, the other a No Entry. Pedestrians flowed both ways down both. And the authorities had capitulated. The No Entry passage had been divided in two by a railing in acquiescence. It's the path theory again, working this time.

The birthday present was bugging me. So I abandoned my plan to cover the rest of the Piccadilly Line and instead jumped on the Victoria Line and headed for Oxford Circus. So much for organisation. Here I was just halfway through the first day and the plan had already gone to pot.

I knew I was abroad when I heard the pipes. There, outside Selfridges, was this fully dressed Highland soldier playing *Cock of the North*. You don't get that in Scotland – except in Edinburgh during the Festival.

I started looking for the present. I could have had a phone that was also a radio for £19.99, or a motorised scooter at £990. There was a talking alarm clock at £16.99. There was a voice organiser, there were big scales, a Marilyn Monro neon radio, a designer kettle, an electric acupuncture machine, a long torch, a very long torch or an infra-red massager. In other words, nothing.

I went down the escalator to bras and then to Turkish carpets. Would she keep one until she got her own flat? Then to belts. Black belts, buckles, white, red, studs, jewels, beige, lurid. Oh God.

Outside, the piper was still playing.

Down to the Bond Street Tube, where there was a beautiful card shop. I headed for Covent Garden and the Transport Museum. I could get an appropriate gift there, and get back on the trail of the Piccadilly Line. A German with a baby in a pram asked for directions. 'Do you know where there is a pub called the Brahms and Liszt?' I showed him my Covent Garden guide which I couldn't read without my glasses. 'No,' he said, 'It is not there. Maybe I have got the wrong spelling.' I didn't try to explain the joke. Cockney

39

rhyming slang would be beyond him. Was someone winding him up? That night I checked in the phone book and, yes, there is such a pub just round the corner, at 19 Russell Street.

My travels were to end for the day at a friend's house in Highgate. I changed to the Northern Line and I now had to look for a phone to find out exactly where I was supposed to go. I discovered that I had no change. Clearly this was the chance to test the theory of the tired, indifferent, commuter. The hypothesis failed, spectacularly. Everyone I asked was helpful. But, despite the combined efforts of three people, we were only able to come up with one coin between us. So I had to get the call right, first time. It was just like holing a birdie putt on the eighteenth.

The phone was answered by a strange voice. My heart sank to my tired feet. Was it a wrong number? No, thank God, it was Jane, the daughter of the house. I now had directions as to where I was supposed to go.

I walked down wooded Muswell Hill Road, with Highgate Wood on one side and Queen's Wood on the other, past a cottage where Peter Sellers used to stay. Next door, a woman was doing something artistic with a frame and thread. She must have been to Cockfosters, too. Close by was another house with a Pavarotti cut-out leaning on the inside window sill and the Christmas decorations still up. What an in-place to live! This, though, was rather spoiled by two girls coming out of a garden flat and one saying to the other, 'It's raining. Fuck.' I hadn't noticed its starting.

The next morning, I retraced my steps back up the hill to Highgate station, just after half past eight. I thought, by that time, I would have avoided the rush hour. But there were still commuters wandering on to the train. So much for the early starts and long journeys all Londoners have to endure. Another myth had been exploded, these people were 20 minutes from the centre. At Highgate station, a busker was tuning his harp and sitting down behind the assortment of chocolates he was offering for sale. Some combination, some class!

I had been wakened at six by the commuters in the house, not all of them worked in Central London, and was tired and out-of-sorts –

exactly as I felt you should be getting on the Tube in the morning.

A quick change at Leicester Square and I was on my way to the other end of the Piccadilly Line and another exotic name – Rayners Lane.

It was a quick change at Leicester Square, mainly because that is not a morning place. But I did miss looking for the Sheriff of Leicester Square – PC Roy Riggs. Referring to the criminals as his clients (they responded by dubbing him the Sheriff), PC Riggs has developed his own uniquely avuncular style of policing one of London's busiest thoroughfares. He talks to the drunks, warns the beggars off, but rugby-tackles the drug pushers. But everything he does, he does with an air of old-world courtesy. 'You can't have the image of the big, hard cop – that just puts people's backs up. You survive by being polite to everybody – even the people you're arresting. That's how you control people, by being civil and gentlemanly.'

I am sorry I missed him.

It was a beautiful day, warm and sunny after an early frost. I was glad when the train burst into the sunlight after Barons Court. The blossom was showing on the trees. 'Frank Dale and Stepsons' the sign just west of Hammersmith proclaimed. Mr Dale and Mr Stepsons? Or Mr Dale and his stepsons? Surely not? 'Small Bills Garage', east of Acton Town, triggered off another absurd thought. Run by a midget?

The good weather cheered me up. I saw the front of the train out of the window. The last time I saw that was when I went by Canadian Pacific through the Rockies. The weather was better today than then. Just the kind of day for a party in a brewery. Not that I was going to get drunk. I don't even drink. But Park Royal meant one thing to me and that was Guinness. I just had to stop here.

In 1759, Arthur Guinness left County Clare for Dublin a rich man. He had just been left £100 in his grandfather's will. A few years later he was worth a fortune. He had used his inheritance to buy a clapped-out brewery in the Irish capital in which he brewed a complicated ale which had to be served by blending several barrels. He then decided to compete with a new English beer popular with the porters of Covent Garden and which English brewers had just introduced to Dublin. Today it seems strange that English brewers and Irish drinkers would unite in such a venture at that time. But then Ireland was firmly under British rule and Dublin was just another city in the United Kingdom.

'Porter' because of the Covent Garden connection, this new beer was also known as 'Entire' because it was served from only one barrel, and was dark from the roasted barley that was used in its production. Guinness was so successful that he was able to start selling it back to England. By 1920, three million barrels of Guinness were being churned out every week, and in 1936 the Park Royal Brewery was opened to take advantage of the demand.

It's not a Royal park in the sense of Epping Forest. It gets its Royal tag from the fact that it was used as a showground by the Royal Agricultural Society. The two oaks growing in front of the main office were planted by Edward VII and his son George V when they visited the Exhibition in 1903.

The building was designed by the architect of Battersea Power Station, Giles Gilbert Scott, in 1933. It was designed to make use of the natural slope on which the buildings stand, so that gravity is used to move the raw materials and the product from one stage to the next. Pure genius.

Next along the line, Alperton seemed such a bland name that I didn't expect to find much there. But this birthday present was bothering me and I just thought I might find a shop. No such luck. So I phoned Mandy. 'Get me something from Harrods,' she suggested. Oh, great. That's like 'get me something distributed by the British retail industry'. No help at all.

I had hoped to travel all the way to Uxbridge and, although people got off at Rayners Lane and waited on the platform for the Uxbridge train, on enquiring of the guard I discovered that the train they were waiting for was on the Metropolitan Line. So it would be cheating to go there on this journey. I would have a quick look round Rayners Lane, but Uxbridge would wait for another day.

There are supposed to be some art deco buildings at Rayners Lane. At least, so Harrow Council's guidebook claims, a claim confirmed by their PR department. But I couldn't see them. Maybe that was my fault. The lack of the birthday present was preventing my concentrating. And now I had the threat of Harrods hanging over me.

But then, for the second time in two days, I broke out of the straight-jacket of my plans. 'I'm on the Tube,' I thought. 'What could be easier?' I suddenly saw the advantage of living in bland Alperton or not-so-art-deco Rayners Lane. These people could just jump on a train and be in the best shop in the world in 15 minutes.

A quarter of an hour later, I arrived at Knightsbridge, and Harrods. I went to the Arcade – an area inside the shop devoted to the kind of gifts tourists would buy. There were Harrods mugs and Harrods towels. Harrods teddies and Harrods soap. Harrods glasses and Harrods picnic baskets. There were Harrods umbrellas. Three different types of Harrods umbrellas. I could have a Harrods coloured walking stick with a bicycle bell on it. For disabled cyclists, I presume. Scots (and others) keep saying that, because of the connection with Livingstone. But did you know that Stanley was ridiculed in the British press for it? Thinking, I presume, that Livingstone was English, he wanted to preserve a front of Victorian cool when his months-long quest came to an end. So he had carefully planned and rehearsed a nonchalant greeting. The English weren't fooled and never let him forget it.

I settled for a Harrods clock and a Harrods mug. Then I went back and changed the clock.

I got my journey back on the Piccadilly track by heading for Hyde Park Corner for a meeting in Lower Belgrave Street. This is a beautiful part of town. The cream terraced houses, with their black doors and brass knockers, epitomise the wealth and sophistication of the inner city dwellers.

My meeting was with a businessman, a tycoon, a captain of industry, a disciple of Thatcher. He was chairman of a company which manufactures condoms. He told me that they made their product in India. A bit surreal. The very place they won't use them. And can you imagine the quality control? It's enough to make you rely on the rhythm method!

I wanted to talk to him about the City in preparation for my tour of the Circle Line. But, on hearing I was writing a book, he insisted that I include the Albert Hall, and we had a far more interesting discussion about London as a cultural capital. He offered me a tour of the Hall. But is it on the Tube? Yes, I was assured. The promenaders walk from South Kensington, a beautiful walk, past some of the most important museums in London.

I promised that I would do that. But first I had to head back east on the Piccadilly Line to Caledonian Road.

It was only when travelling by Tube to lunch, poring over the map, that I realised that Caledonian Road would have been a great place for a Scotsman to start his pilgrimage to the English – and British – capital. In winter, I suspect, Caledonian Road could well be a bleak and windswept part of London. In early spring, it was actually hot, crying out for an ice-cream van to tinkle its way into your consciousness. Emerging from its rather dirty, dated, underground station, with its sludgy-browny-purple glazed tile frontage, is a little disorientating. All around you is the rather hideous London brick, not quite yellow, pretending to be mellow, and managing to give a harsh, unyielding face to the townscape. But Caledonian Road, apart from sounding Scottish, offered a sense of the real London – not the tourist traps or the showpieces, but the unadulterated experience of ordinary people going about their daily lives.

I was beginning to catch my breath after a hurried start to my journeys, settling into the pace. I wandered slowly round the district, browsing for feeling, for atmosphere and for inspiration. I stepped out into the not-so-fresh air of Caledonian Road. Opposite was the Cally Bingo Hall. Down the road, the Cally Congregational Church, and the Cally Pool. Not quite a theme park, but all of a kind. And the classic blue lamp outside the police station. I looked around for Jack Warner. But all I saw was a dog with an all-over afro, its hair the same dirty brown colour as its owner.

Tom and Angie run the Caledonian Road Flower Shop. Tom's an Essex man settled here in Islington, but he seemed pretty aware of the Scottish connections. Angie, a large woman, was sitting at her computer gazing at her sales figures on the screen – even flower shops, these days, are computerised it seems. Just round the corner, she told me, is MacKenzie Road, and Lockhart Close – not the kind of close you get in Glasgow (a common staircase for six or eight tenement flats), but flats nevertheless, in a 1980s cul-de-sac housing development. Across the road and round the corner in Market Street is Highland House, another Eighties development in yellow brick and concrete, a hopeful and slightly out-of-place corporate palace. It's small wonder it's empty.

Market Street leads to what is now Caledonian Park, a pretty desultory open space fringed by overgrown shrubs and the odd tree – attempting to mask the adjacent council flats which are their own tribute to unimaginative architecture but which, thankfully, are being remodelled. A fleet of heavy-trailered lorries arrived, bringing an incipient fairground to the spot. The area is enclosed by a magnificent set of substantial railings, with massive cast-iron pillars, which give a hint of something more interesting in the past. Indeed, that past is even more evident by the structure which dominates the space – a four-square and ornate clock tower in the Italianate style, about 60 feet tall. And, though there was evidence at ground level of vandalism and the ever-present paint sprayers, the clock still works.

At the entrance to the park, beside the heavy iron gates, there was a historical display board. Its plastic front had been thickly sprayed with black paint, making it difficult to decipher what was behind. But I managed to discern that the clock tower was all that remained of the Caledonian Market which had been established on the site of the former Copenhagen House. This was, evidently, an impressive country mansion, built in the seventeenth century either to accommodate the Danish ambassador during the Great Plague in London or to house Danish royalty visiting James VI; or James I, as they say in England. No one down here will ever understand the furore caused in Scotland when the present monarch succeeded to the throne as Elizabeth II: her namesake predecessor was, of course, an enemy of Scotland, not its ruler. And Scotland knew no other Elizabeth, so how could this one be the second? In Scotland, Royal Mail post boxes and post vans still carry only a crown, not the initials and number of the monarch. The Scots tended to blow up those that did.

Of Copenhagen House there is not a trace, because the City of London bought the site in 1852 and built a cattle market to replace Smithfield. It was located here because it was on the drove road from the north. At its peak, it catered for 42,000 sheep and 7,000 cattle on market day, not to mention pigs and calves. The market operated on Mondays and Thursdays, after which, on Fridays, it was a festering breeding ground for a flea market. The clock tower kept everyone on time.

But Smithfield proved resilient and, in the early part of the twentieth century, the Caledonian Market declined and was taken over by the antiques trade. Later, that, too, moved – according to Tom – to Bermondsey, where there is now a well-established *bric–a–brac* market. Now, the only antique left at Caledonian Park is the clock tower, looking ludicrously isolated and abandoned in its unsympathetic environment. The display board proudly told me about the wildlife which inhabited the park. All I could see were hordes of unruly children and a scattering of semi-naked bodies was already on the grass, soaking in the hot spring sun. I couldn't linger fully-clothed, and London can live without my nakedness. So I turned and wandered back towards the underground station – past something obscure to do with the unknown University of North London. This is a label now apparently pinned to every educational building in a vast urban fall-out area north of the Thames. But this one seemed to be empty, unlike the adjacent privately run Emile Woolf accountancy training college, which was overflowing with students from the New Commonwealth.

One of the most striking things about wandering around unlikely parts of London is the number of universities that have sprouted up. The Student Loans Company lists 28 universities with London postal addresses. About 24 too many, I'd say. Not that I don't believe in universal education, but I simply refuse to believe that we have an unlimited supply of brains to fill all of these new places at that level of education. And that's just to speak of the teachers. Why can't people be content to go to polys or to technical colleges? Is anyone but the new graduand going to believe that a degree from the University of North London or Westminster is equivalent to one from Glasgow or Oxford?

Scots have a strange attitude to London. In the tradition of love–hate relationships, it is not entirely unhealthy. But it does permeate their view of England as a whole, a view often too flattering to many other parts of that diverse kingdom of which it is atypical. London is the capital of the capitalists. It is still, even in these turbulent days for the monarchy, the Royal seat of the English Royals. And London is, above all, the centre of government for Great Britain, the location of the British civil service, and the attendant head-office mentality with all its self-centredness and general ignorance of the needs of the rest of the country. It is not a coincidence that the Underground system stops at Watford. Londoners have long believed that this was the end of the line.

Yet London is unquestionably a magnificent city. Its institutions, its public buildings, its spacious parks, its expensive shops, its self-contained villages and its cosmopolitan population all reek of justified self-importance. Whereas in Los Angeles you feel that you have been catapulted by jet liner into the future, in London you feel at the centre of the here and now. London is essential viewing for all foreign visitors.

Shared by Londoners and visitors to London alike is the city's Underground system. This is more-or-less uniquely a twentieth-century creation, for – although the shallow lines of the inner Metropolitan, District and Circle systems were first started in the late Victorian era – it wasn't until they were electrified and incorporated into the unified Electric Railways Company of London Limited that real commercial progress could be made. This happened in April 1902.

Thereafter, the system grew like Topsy in all directions – in some cases following the sprawling suburbs and in others – most famously the line to John Betjeman's 'Metroland', the Metropolitan Line from Paddington to Watford Junction – leading and enabling the development of new residential areas.

Unlike the 'cut and cover' of the original constructions in central London, the new lines were excavated at great depth, the tunnels lined with metal. Thus the 'Tube' came into existence, and with it some mind-boggling statistics about 'the deepest station', 'the longest tunnel' and 'the tallest escalator'.

By the time London made its first serious attempt at an integrated transport system with the creation of the London Passenger Transport Board in 1933, the Tube had been firmly established by private enterprise as the fastest and most convenient method of getting about the city state.

Indeed, a whole new city had become established underneath the surface city. Not just the Underground, but a Victorian water and sewerage system which was – and still is – the envy of the world, once-open rivers, and a range of private physical communications passages and postal and telecommunications tunnels for the General Post Office, and a network of 'secret' bunkers and caverns earmarked for emergencies and governments in time of war. No wonder that London, and the British government, survived the worst ravages to the surface which Hitler could devise. Nowhere else in the world were alternative arrangements so complete, or so effective. Londoners took to their prepared burrows like country moles.

The London Underground has a history of continuous additions and extensions, and these continued after World War Two. At their outermost fringes, all the lines came to the surface and were extended to their new terminal points. But, until the 1960s, no new tubes had been started for more than 50 years. The Victoria Line, opened in 1969, was therefore a major adventure, with new technology giving rise to the possibility of driverless trains. Understandably perhaps from their point of view, the transport unions campaigned to prevent this happening on the Victoria Line from the start, but Luddites have always lacked imagination or confidence in the future and are fortunately but fleeting phenomena. The subsequent development and operation of the Jubilee Line, opened ten years later, has proved that there are no limits to the improvements which could be made to what is already one of the most effective transportation systems on the planet.

As the Jubilee Line thrusts new tubes eastwards to link up with the new Docklands developments, the Underground must be reaching its geographical limits. But the system is likely to go rapidly out of date if sufficient investment is not forthcoming for the renewal of existing lines. And who will sanction that? Is the market really able to assess the long term, wider benefits to the community of expanding and modernising such a social asset? I doubt it. By the time the latest extension to the Jubilee Line is complete, there will be a total of 365 stations on nine lines. And that doesn't count the Docklands Light Railway, which has assumed an independent appetite for expansion all on its own.

I turned back into the womb of Caledonian Road underground station organising my thoughts. Because that was about all the preparation my expedition round the rest of the Underground was going to need. It didn't call for the kind of planning that requires the packing of the right clothes, or an adequate amount of food or medical supplies. I didn't need injections or malaria tablets. I wouldn't even have to book the transport or the hotels. I didn't need a short wave radio, much less a transmitter. The territory was familiar enough not to have to worry about a map – and, anyway, there was one in every station. So, I couldn't get lost. But I did have to get foreign currency. The machines on the Tube have an aversion to Scottish notes – especially pound ones. But on the resources front that was about all that was necessary.

Not that this was necessarily an advantage. How many great travel tales have you read where the preparations take up about 14 chapters in flash-back in the middle of the book when the traveller discovers that he has forgotten his third change of underpants? I'd done it all in a paragraph. And I would be going home to change my underpants.

But the project hadn't really started in Caledonian Road. And it hadn't started with a plan, but with an impulse. This visit was an attempt to impose a coherence on that exuberant decison.

So I had as much to think about as I stepped on to my train as Scott had as he boarded *Discovery*. I remembered what had caused his undoing. He refused to force his dogs to undergo the hardships that he and his team so willingly embraced, and walked on to his death. There and then, I determined that I certainly wasn't going to allow any false sentimentality about animals to prevent me from completing my epic voyage. If it came to it, I would eat anything – as long as someone else had killed it and made it into a burger.

But before continuing the journey, I must tell you something more about the Piccadilly Line. First of all, it is a Great American Invention. Well, not exactly an invention. But it does owe it origins to an American entrepreneur with a chequered history.

Charles Tyson Yerkes was born of Quaker parentage in Philadelphia in 1839. Although his father was a bank president, Charles went to work at 15, earning only his keep for the first year. At 21, he became a broker on the local stock exchange. Almost immediately, he became involved in some murky business over municipal bonds, buying and selling frantically with the connivance of the city treasurer to keep their price up. In 1871, the great fire of Chicago, which started with Mrs O'Leary's cow knocking over an oil lamp and ended with the homelessness of more than 100,000 people and the destruction of more than half the city, caused panic in eastern money markets. Yerkes could not meet his obligations. Convicted of misappropriating funds, he was sent to the state penitentiary for 33 months. His friends didn't forget him, however, and a petition to the Governor of Pennsylvania, signed by various bankers and brokers, gained his release after seven months.

Needing to restore his fortune, he set up the Continental Passenger Railway and sent the share price up from $15 to $100. Another failure wiped out everybody but him.

Moving with a fortune of $40,000 to Chicago in 1881, he wheeled and dealed as a stock and grain broker until, in 1886, he secured control of the North Chicago City Railway. This was the beginning of a new career which saw him bribe his way into obtaining, for no financial return to the city, 100–year franchises to operate trams in Chicago. Most of the local politicians were in his pocket. But he couldn't buy the Governor – possibly because he was too expensive – who vetoed the renewal of the franchises in 1895. Yerkes campaigned against him, and caused him to lose the next election. Only mass meetings – and a march by irate citizens brandishing guns and nooses – prevented the new administration from renewing his franchises. One of the marchers' grudges was that many of them could never get a seat on his trams. But that was deliberate policy. 'It's the strap-hangers who pay the dividends,' he argued.

Yerkes left Chicago in 1899, after having disposed of his holdings for $20 million. Before he said his farewells to the United States, he had presented its people with the finest astronomical telescope in the world. He then headed for England, where he became a pioneer of Tube railways. He bought the District Line in 1900, and then gradually took over every other line in London except the Metropolitan. He wasn't really interested in trains. But, as only an embezzler with a prison record could, he recognised a good financial investment.

He also built the Lot's Road power station in Chelsea, which still supplies the system with nearly half of its electric juice. The rest comes from the Greenwich power station. Between them, they have a generating capacity of 280 megawatts, which is probably enough to power every television set in Britain.

Yerkes already owned the District Line when he put up the cash for the original Piccadilly line, which was opened in December 1906, a year after his death.

The first stretch was a nine-and-half-mile tunnel from Finsbury Park to Barons Court, which then came up for air all the way to Hammersmith. That was it until the 1930s, when the line was extended to South Harrow, Hounslow West and Uxbridge to the west; and first to Arnos Grove and then to Cockfosters in the east in 1933.

The Heathrow extension came in 1977, so that the line now covers over 43 miles and serves 53 stations, using 73 trains. The trains were bought in 1973 and have extra space in each carriage for the luggage that a train serving an airport must expect passengers to carry.

There is still a service which runs at peak hours between Holborn and Aldwych, but this is likely to close because the lifts at Aldwych would cost £3 million to repair. They haven't done badly, though. They're 87 years old!

The Piccadilly Line holds the record for the shortest distance between two stations – 0.16 of a mile between Leicester Square and Covent Garden. That is by rail. It is, of course, quicker to walk between these two.

Here and at one or two other places on the Underground system, you can win lots of bets challenging the uninitiated to a race between stations, as long as you can make the choice of stations. Pick, say, Euston Square on the Circle and Warren Street on the Victoria. Your victims are allowed to take the Tube while you have to go by foot. In this case, they will find that they have to travel all the way to King's Cross just to change lines, while you can have a full English breakfast, a haircut or a manicure and saunter off to stand inside one station with your hand out for your winnings as they emerge panting from the other just across the road.

London's like that. So is its Underground.

CHAPTER THREE

FIRST AND FAR AWAY

For the most famous of all underground lines, it could be a bit of an embarrassment to admit that only six of the Metropolitan's 41 miles are in fact underground. But that is par for the course for the whole system. Only 105 miles are underground. Twenty of these are cut and cover and 85 are in tubes. The other 139 miles which complete the system are overground.

The Metropolitan Line carries this anomaly with greater panache than most. Because, when the first section opened on 10 January 1863, although it only ran for three and three-quarters miles from Paddington to Farringdon, London became the first city in the world to have an underground railway.

It was, like all the early lines, a private sector venture. The company had great difficulty in the early years of the project, and it might well have been totally abandoned had it not been for 'the well-founded and universal outcry at the impediments to circulation in London arising from the mighty tide of traffic passing through it'.

On the opening day, it was calculated that more than 30,000 persons were carried over the line in the course of the day. Indeed, the desire to travel this line from day one was more than the directors had provided for. From nine o'clock in the morning until past midday it was impossible to obtain a place in the up or cityward line at any of the mid stations.

In the evening, the tide turned, and the crush at the Farringdon Street station was as great as the doors of a theatre on the first night of some popular performer. Some lightening of the pressure was obtained by the Great Western lending some of their engines and carriages supplemental to the rolling stock of the company. Notwithstanding the throng, no accident

*occurred, and the report of the passengers was unanimous in
favour of the smoothness and comfort of the line.*

So wrote the compiler of the Annual Register for the year in
which the line was opened, 1863. Eighteen sixty–three. Queen
Victoria was 48 and had been on the throne 26 years. Palmerston was
Prime Minister. The American Civil War was moving into its third
year and Lincoln would need only 268 words immortally to define
democracy with the delivery of the Gettysburg Address.

It was to be another 45 years before the name 'Underground' was
adopted on all stations within the system, and another five years
before they got round to inventing the famous logo, while in 1916
Edward Johnston designed a special typeface for the Underground,
which is still in use.

The Metropolitan Line trains seem bigger, more important. The
seats all face forwards and backwards, like grown-up trains, not
sideways. The one I was on also sounded like a bigger train. And it
rattled more. I attributed all of this to illusion. I had started out
personifying the lines. And now I was trying to detect different
characteristics between the different trains.

Later I discovered from Caroline (there's an appropriate name) at
the Underground's headquarters that there had always been two
types of train, 'surface' and 'tube'. 'Surface' trains run on the older
parts of the system which, if underground at all, are very near the
surface having been built by the 'cut and cover' method of digging
a ditch and covering it over. This includes the Metropolitan Line, of
course, and the District, Circle, Hammersmith and City and East
London lines. And the trains that run on these lines *are* bigger than
those that run on the Tube lines – Bakerloo, Central, Jubilee,
Northern, Piccadilly and Victoria.

The unpainted aluminium–bodied trains that I always thought of
as Tube trains – because they ran on the Piccadilly Line from
Heathrow – were, in fact, restricted to that line and the Central. The
Metropolitan Line trains date from 1960, but they are being given a
major refurbishment by 1997. On other lines, brand new rolling
stock is being introduced. The latest of these are full-length
advertising hoardings – the one for United Airlines on the Piccadilly
being the very first.

It seemed right to start my Metropolitan journey from one of its original stations. Most of them have been hijacked by upstart lines like the Hammersmith and City. So I settled on Baker Street, from where the modern Metropolitan Line heads confidently northwards in tandem with what is now part of the Jubilee Line, the youngest of the system. The two lines consent to exchange passengers at Finchley Road and Wembley Park. My first essential destination was Wembley Park, whose station opened in 1923.

I had not visited there since the 1977 England–Scotland game. Then, I had arrived in an overcrowded train from Central London. That trip was notorious for the molestation and near-rape of two girls who had boarded a train loaded with 'loaded' Scots. The girls had, quite understandably, failed to realise that joining in the banter would be mistaken for an invitation. It was sickening to see their high spirits being misinterpreted by a horde of wild and irresponsible fans.

Today, the train was hardly half full and my fellow passengers this time were docile and respectable commuters. Wembley had changed quite dramatically, too. Olympic Way, or Wembley Way as we Scots in our ignorance called it, had been pedestrianised and a new traffic flow system introduced. The underpass was tiled with sportsmen and women – presumably from the range of sports that Wembley catered for. The Way was lined with official souvenir booths and fast food stalls, all very American.

I mentioned my ignorance of the correct address. Wembley Stadium has many ways, but not a Wembley one. There is an Olympic Way, a Stadium Way, an Empire Way, South Way, a Great Central Way, and, curiously, a Lakeside Way. Thereafter the city fathers ran out of ideas. Other streets are called First Way, Second Way, Third Way, Fourth Way and Fifth Way. Oddly, a tiny street called Wembley Way is half a mile away in Tokyngton, with no direct road access and separated from the stadium by British Rail. But here, surely, is a great opportunity for some positive public relations by the local council: a Matthews Way, a Finney Way, and so on? And 'No Way' would provoke a smile.

In 1967, I had arranged to meet friends outside the stadium. I was dressed very conservatively in a suit, collar and tie and a smart overcoat – my tartan scarf discreetly tucked inside: a Scotland fan, but deeply atypical. Wembley, on the day of a big game, was then a hard place to get anything to eat. There were very few restaurants, the pubs overflowed and 'take-away' or 'carry-out' as a concept had yet to be imported from Scotland. So I went into a grocer's and bought a pie and a pint of milk. I stood outside eating and drinking – only to be derided by a gang of fellow Scots chanting 'Spot the Looney'. Being a man of principle, I ditched the milk.

Today, I walked around the perimeter of the stadium to appreciate the comprehensiveness of the Wembley complex – the arena, the Sunday market, the conference centre. But, if Sir Edward Watkins' dream had been fulfilled, all of this would have been clustered round, not the hallowed turf, but the Wembley Tower. Sir Edward was chairman of the company that owned the Metropolitan Line. Like many entrepreneurs, most of whom succeed by luck, he attributed his financial success to talent and decided to turn his flair to the tourist industry. He planned to build, right in the middle of the pitch, which was not yet there, of course, a rival to the Eiffel Tower. An international competition was launched with a prize of 500 guineas to find the best design.

In 1890, a Scottish firm, Stewart, McLaren and Dunn, won the commission with a design that was 190 feet higher than its French rival. It was built up to the first stage. Sir Edward, drawing on all his railway experience and anxious to get the cash flowing as soon as possible, insisted that the bit that was built be opened to the public. But towers are not like railway lines. The public weren't interested in this half-built marvel and never came in any numbers. The funding for the next phase never materialised and the tower was demolished in 1907. It's another version of the Law of Diminishing Returns: there's a lot less than half the attraction in half an attraction.

I had been attracted by a mysterious building shown on my map, and which, therefore, must surely have been built. It was identified as Mahatma Gandhi House. It was at the far side of the stadium from the station. Unfortunately, I misread the map and walked about a mile in the wrong direction before I discovered my mistake. My feet had begun to hurt. And there is nothing that concentrates your attention on sore feet more than losing your way.

I retraced the bloodstains and found the Red House, which, unbelievably, was the headquarters of the local Tories. Next to it was my destination, Mahatma Gandhi House. What would it be? An institute devoted to peace studies? Part of the Indian High Commission?

To my intense disappointment, it is Brent Council's Housing Services Department. If it had been Nelson Mandela House, I would not have been fooled. But the name that they had chosen to honour was an echo of a bygone era.

In my disappointment, and to rest my feet, I struggled into the adjacent Hilton Hotel. In the lounge which looks out over Mahatma Gandhi House, I studied the menu. The great leader was a vegetarian, so I decided to avoid the meat dishes. But he was also an ascetic who would baulk at paying £5.30 for Avocado, Apple and Walnut Salad 'with selected choice of varied lettuce and leaves'. I don't know whether he approved of stimulants, but he would not have wanted to pay £2.50 for a pot of tea either. In deference to the Mahatma, I left without buying anything.

I walked back to the station, past the industrial estate with its art deco frontages, to seek out the Palace of Arts. Betjeman's description, 'massive and simple outside, almost pagan in its sombre strength', *demanded* that I find it. But it had been demolished. The facade is still there. But the poet's description is now its epitaph.

I continued my journey north-westwards, observing briefly that the Preston Road station must have been so named because there is nothing there more interesting after which to name the station. Northwick Park looked more enticing, but I was anxious to get to the next station, so passed up the opportunity to explore.

At first sight, Harrow-on-the-Hill seems like any typical London suburb. There is a McDonald's and a Pizza Hut close by the station. But the hyphens in the name hinting at exclusivity do not deceive. This place reeks class. And it reeks of the class system. Where better place to start the search for this than on the playing fields of Harrow School, which I assume fulfilled the same decisive role at Waterloo as those of Eton?

The decision to go in that direction meant sacrificing a visit to Grove Hill, a couple of hundred yards in the opposite direction. Here, it is claimed, 'the first fatal motor accident involving the driver petrol driven car' occurred. Had he forgotten his red flag that day?

Instead, I walked briskly down Kenton Road into Watford Road. 'It's time to plant hanging baskets', announced a hanging sign outside the Plantation Garden Centre. This was not, thank goodness, a pun exploiting the nearby Tyburn Lane. It was a horticultural exhortation to the middle class. And naturally, in Harrow, they had got the apostrophe in the right place in the 'it's'. Not many people can do that now. Churchill claimed that parsing sentences was the source of his mastery of language. And he learned it at Harrow.

I found myself walking past the Harrow Hill Golf Course, which the map more accurately describes as 'pitch and putt'. The nine holes were totally deserted and the Portakabin pro shop showed no sign of life. But the notice said 'Open'.

I could do with the practice. All of this travelling was doing nothing to allow me to maintain my tenuous hold on a 21 handicap. If they hired clubs, I could practise my short game. But this is London. It would be expensive. Well, I would pay £10 for a round. I decided to check it out. The PGA pro, Simon Bishop, was not in. But lurking in the gloom of the hut was his assistant, Peter, engrossed in the *Sun*. Yes, I could hire clubs at £1 for an iron and a putter. Nine holes were £3. But balls were sold not rented. They would cost 60p each. Even by Scottish standards, this was cheap.

I went outside to digest this information. I could do with the practice. But I wouldn't be playing with my own clubs. These borrowed ones might upset my swing. And putting on what looked like very uneven greens might make my putting even worse. And shoes. I had no golf shoes, and if I started slipping around in my ordinary brogues, I might upset my rhythm completely – especially as my feet had not got any less sore. No, the more I thought about it, this practice idea might set me back months. Golf is a game of the mind, I reminded myself. So that, after I had concluded these mental exercises, I realised that they would stand me in enormous stead the next time that I stood on the first tee. I would remember all the faults that practising here would have produced. I would remember that, despite the temptation, I had decided *not* to practise. And I would be in the right frame of mind to play well.

Anyway, looking at the score card, rule two of the local rules stated: 'When the flag is removed, it must be laid lightly on the green, and not stuck in the turf'. What kind of barbarians played here? No Scot would comprehend the need to put that in writing.

After all, we invented the game. Or rather we didn't, the Dutch did. And their sailors brought it to Scotland through Leith. But we don't acknowledge that. And neither does anyone else because the Dutch are so pathetically bad at national public relations. Proof of that? Well, for example, they insist on retaining a flag that is indistinguishable from that of France, or Luxembourg or half of the bits of former Yugoslavia. It's that kind of disregard for image and marketing that allows us to get the kudos for golf, and the golfing tourists.

The Harrow playing fields are set firmly behind a three-deep phalanx of trees which screen them totally from the busy Watford Road. But these are not playing fields. This is a public park. Private park? No, if Harrow is a public school this must be a public park. At any rate, at 300 acres it is bigger than Lampton Park (44½ acres) which serves the 206,000 people of Hounslow and Ravenscourt Park (34 acres) put together.

This park is for the exclusive use of 674 boys. That might be 675 boys. The school archivist couldn't quite remember. He did remember that there were no girls in the school. Not that they are barred. They are admitted to sixth year. It's just that there aren't any there at the moment.

When the 674 or 5 boys have finished working out on their 300 acres, they can repair to the adjacent Harrow School farm to help the farm labourers keep fit by directing them in their physical tasks, just as their fathers and grandfathers did before them. This also reinforces their natural leadership tendencies.

I walked back into town and up Peterborough Road, past huge houses with names like *The Garlands* and *Heathfield*, to the school.

They know how to do things properly, these aristocrats. This place is charming. Quaint, narrow streets with few cars, clean red brick buildings, luxuriant gardens. The school has class. The little village is crammed with art galleries and antique shops. The pub is called the King's Head. It dates from 1535 and the king shown is Henry VIII. I wonder what they called it in the time of Charles I, or rather, after the time of Charles I when such a name would surely have been considered a sick joke?

In the middle of the High Street, right across from the school, is an elegant *restaurant français* called the Old Etonian.

'Why did you call it that?' I asked its owner.

'It's obvious,' he answered. 'If I had called it the Old Harrovian, you wouldn't have asked.'

'Were you at Eton then?' I asked.

'Yes,' he said.

'When?' I asked.

'Last year, for lunch.'

He enjoyed a good relationship with the boys, he said, who loved the name. I'm sure they did. It's the kind of one-upmanship that they just *have* to learn.

On the outside of the bigger houses were peculiar signs, *Flambards, Moretons, Druries, Rendalls.* On the wall of Harrow School Suppliers was a plaque that seemed to refer to the clock above the shop. But the Latin was too much for me, although years of watching film and TV credits enabled me to decipher the year as 1952 – far too modern to worry about. Simpler was the school motto on the blazer in the window of the Harrow School Outfitters, *Stet Fortuna Domus,* – in *good* English, according to the archivist, 'God Bless this House'. The school colours are rather like the Scotland rugby ones – a dark blue and white. In the window was everything from jogging suits to tail-coats, green waistcoats to straw boaters. And, of course, cricket sweaters for use in that public park down the hill.

I walked on to the rolling lawn in front of the main school building and looked out back at the panorama of central London. In doing so, I inadvertently got my photograph taken with a group of Taiwanese visitors.

Back out past the Bursar's Office, I tentatively rang the general enquiries bell of the Old House. I did not expect an answer and was not disappointed. It just did not seem that they would be the kind of people to be 'in' to casual visitors. Next door is the school book-shop, formerly a house where Robert Peel boarded. It boasted a biography of Winston Churchill, naturally. And *Hitler and Stalin – Parallel Lives.* And the *Oxford Companion to the Second World War.* At £30, what schoolboy could afford that? These ones, obviously.

And yet, when the school was founded in 1571 by John Lyon,

who set aside 20 marks (we were nearer to a single European currency then), it was for the education of the poor children of Harrow. It continued to serve this purpose until 1660 when a cunning headmaster discovered a loophole in John Lyon's statute, through which he admitted 'foreigners', i.e. paying pupils from outside the parish. The parishioners of Harrow woke up to this just 149 years later and took the school to court. But the Court of Chancery threw their case out. So the poor were not always with them.

Walking back past the school church, which was padlocked shut, I saw two plaques. One told me that the original building was completed in 1615. The other was to commemorate Anthony Ashley Cooper, later seventh Earl of Shaftesbury KG.

Near this spot Cooper, while yet a boy at Harrow School, saw with shame and indignation the pauper's funeral which helped to awaken his life-long devotion to the service of the poor and the oppressed.

Of all the pupils who had ever been to Harrow, was he the only one who had ever shown a concern for the poor? Otherwise, why weren't there hundreds of plaques? But it is a nice touch.

The Earl of Shaftesbury entered Parliament for his family seat of Dorset and was associated with much of the nineteenth century factory legislation. He was a philanthropist who chaired many of London's charitable societies. His progressive ideas must have been influenced by memories of the first earl, one Anthony Ashley Cooper. It was a surprisingly unimaginative family; all the earls were called Anthony Ashley Cooper. Anyway, the first earl, during the Civil War, raised a troop for the King. But, as the dispute wore on, he began increasingly to take Parliament's side. Indeed, he is now credited as being one of the earliest advocates of parliamentary democracy. Our earl, however, did not allow this, or his concern for the poor, to carry him away. He naturally held on to all his titles and privileges. And he also managed to bring himself to vote against the Great Reform Bill of 1832 which extended the franchise in a very limited way.

He may well have been aware that reforming by example can often lead to unacceptable consequences. Tolstoy was so horrified by the concept of bondage that he freed his hundreds of serfs, throwing them out of work and into destitution. His action also imposed an unbearable burden on his wife whom he expected to lavish huge banquets on the guests he still insisted on inviting to the house.

But Shaftesbury has left his mark: London's poor were so impressed with the seventh earl's social conscience that they erected Eros in Piccadilly Circus to his glory.

There was another famous Harrovian in the House of Commons at the same time, Lord Palmerston. He voted for the Great Reform Bill – as a result of which the electors of his seat, the University of Cambridge, threw him out!

In the churchyard of the 900-year-old St Mary's Church, there is the tomb on which Byron used to lie to write poetry. Far more interesting is the slate tomb of Mrs Mary Port, one of the first victims of a railway crash. She didn't travel too well.

I walked back down the public footpath through the playing fields, just to be sure that I hadn't over-estimated their size. No, they still looked like the prairies.

As I walked back to the Tube station, I noticed a polythene-clad building on Watford Road. This was the University of Westminster, Harrow Campus, previously Harrow College. I'll bet there is no boy sweating over his textbooks up the hill desperate to drum up enough passes to scrape into this particular institution.

Not that Harrow would expect a student's aspiration to enter an academic institution to be inhibited by performance in examinations. Winston Churchill tells how he could answer no questions at all on the Latin paper that would determine whether he entered Harrow or not. He records that he simply 'wrote down the number of the question "I". After much reflection I put a bracket round it thus "(I)". But thereafter I could not think of anything connected with it that was either relevant or true.'

But from 'these slender indications of scholarship, [the headmaster] drew the conclusion that I was worthy to pass into Harrow'. The fact that Churchill's father had only just resigned as Leader of the House of Commons and Chancellor of the Exchequer was neither here nor there.

Incidentally, Churchill was a regular Tube traveller when he was in his twenties. He notes in the first part of his memoirs, 'I was able to live with my mother (in Grosvenor Square) and go down to Hounslow Barracks two or three times a week by the Underground Railway.'

Child of the First War, Forgotten by the Second
We called you Metro-land. We laid our schemes
Lured by the lush brochure, down byways beckoned,
To build at last the cottage of our dreams,
A city clerk turned countryman again,
And linked to the Metropolis by train.

John Betjeman

I was now going to travel as quickly as possible to the end of this particular branch of the Metropolitan Line, at Watford. Betjeman had already made this part of the line immortal, and I could not better his approach.

The signpost outside Watford station indicated that it was one mile to the town centre. The other Tube station, Watford High Street, was on the Bakerloo line, discontinued since 1982. But you can still get there by British Rail if you can't walk the extra mile.

There was no evidence of a taxi service, and buses seemed none too frequent. It was a lovely day, as were most days that summer, so I decided to walk. As everywhere in the suburbs where the Tube disgorged me, I was struck by the high quality of the houses. You can tell the cost of the house by the kind of car that is sitting in the drive. There is a strong correlation between a BMW 5 Series and a £250,000 house or a 20-year-old Mark Ten Jag and a council flat.

The main road carried signs indicating the M1. This was where it all ended. This was the pale. 'North of Watford' is the phrase which signifies Londoners' belief that their city contains all of British culture and, indeed, civilisation. I wondered if the phrase had gained currency after the Metropolitan Line had pushed London's northern boundary to the limit. But apparently not. According to Watford District Council, long before the age of trains, Watford 'was a convenient stopping place for Londoners going north. Hence the expression to denote the boundary between north and south'. The fact that Watford is only 20 miles from Trafalgar Square, and some

300 from the Scottish border, says something about the insularity of the southern English. Or maybe it says everything about the richness and diversity of their city. Even this early on in my travels, London was winning me over.

Watford had always had a heavy sound to me. It sounded dull and dreary, boring and fairly downmarket. The name comes from the Saxon meaning 'a ford used for hunting', which rather says it all. The modern equivalent, given the way that leisure activities are becoming more and more sedentary, might be 'a building used for drinking, a pub'. The Peace Hospital sign outside a wrecked former Hertfordshire Health Authority building confirmed my expectations. Here was another outpost of the looney left. But it turned out to be only a day-care centre in a couple of Portakabins. And it was no indication at all of the kind of place Watford is.

The town itself was an interesting surprise. It is prosperous, clean and safe. It has a hint of the rural about it, right down to horse droppings on the pavement of Rickmansworth Road. If this was public relations, it was highly sophisticated. I was politely and efficiently served in the council office where I sought local information. I walked up the pedestrianised High Street, looking for somewhere to have lunch.

There was an immediate attraction to Yates Wine Lodge because of its advertisement – 'Famous for our Fortified Wines'. What Glaswegian could resist that? But it had not yet opened for business. So I chose the Artichoke instead. It boasted 'Home-made Fayre of the Finest Distinction' on the blackboard outside. Inside, the low-beamed ceiling and range of hunting and shooting prints created the right atmosphere for someone looking for a traditional English pub. But the food didn't match.

'What's in your breakfast?' I asked the cook-cum-waitress.

'We don't serve breakfast this late.'

'But your sign, here, right here above my head says "Breakfast served all day" .'

'That's an old sign,' was the curt response.

I ordered cauliflower and broccoli pie and a cappuccino and left quickly, despite my feet. I had already walked miles that day, and my feet had begun to emit throbbing signals. I knew that they were already blistered. But I didn't want to look. For one thing, there was nothing I could do. And there's a big difference between knowing they are blistered and seeing the devastation with your own eyes. If I looked at my feet, I knew I wouldn't walk another step.

So I carried on back to the station. This time I cut through Cassiobury Park. This is a magnificent affair. And there is acre upon acre of it. It's almost as big as Harrow School's playing fields. Or so I thought. When I checked I discovered that it is, in fact, a third smaller.

I picked up the horse droppings here. Metaphorically, that is. The wooded park opened up into an open field strewn with the aftermath of a funfair. The caravans and trailers stood in a disorganised circle with the expensive rides dismantled and packed, huddled under a flat African-shaped coniferous tree – a testament to the south's gentle climate. There had evidently also been a gymkhana, hence the horse manure. The fairground kids played around on their bikes. One wee girl of about ten silently shot me at point blank range with her rifle. No political correctness among these parents. Or maybe there was, because it was the daughter that had the gun, not her wee brother, who merely looked on.

From the top of the hill, I saw a bridge and walked down to the river it crossed. Here, the River Gade was slow, picturesque, dark and dangerous. It was a scene so typically English. There was the wandering water, the placid ducks, the weeping willows, the green rushes. But the river, whose depth I could not gauge, must have worried the parents whose children would love to play here. Walking along the banks, I came across the council's answer. They had built the best outdoor municipal paddling pool that I had seen in a long time. It wasn't one pool. It was three, each with a sparkling fountain in the middle. There were five little pavilions, modelled loosely on the clubhouse of the Dubai golf club, presumably based on a nomad's tent. These were the changing rooms and toilets. The place was packed with mothers chatting and kids shrilly paddling.

Further on, there was another bridge – and beyond that another bigger, higher bridge over the Grand Union Canal, its boats working their way through the Ironbridge Lock. Cassiobury Park contains a nature reserve with old watercress beds, wetlands and woodland habitats. These, I was given to understand, are important for bird, plant and invertebrates. The picturesque scene was rather spoiled by a notice on the bridge warning of the danger of contracting water-borne diseases in the canal.

Braving this unlikely hazard was a group of boys on the bridge over the River Gade. Their supervisor told me that it was not a school class but a play scheme, organised to keep them out of mischief during the holidays. Today they were fish–spotting, he said. As I watched, a golden retriever ran into the river. The joke rippled through the group, repeated again and again as the boys refused to give up a good line until they had done it to death: 'Look, a dog-fish'.

Watford is one of the many suburban Tube stations which is somewhat remote from the town centre. Unlike mainline stations, the Tube at Watford and High Barnet and Stanmore, for example, land you right in the middle of douce housing schemes. Presumably the Tube generated the houses and they multiplied to join the nearest earlier settlements.

At any rate it makes for a long walk, and my feet were getting more and more painful. On top of which I discovered that I had twisted my knee, which was making walking even more of an effort. But I had set myself a schedule and this time, after my two previous failures, I was determined to fulfil it. So it was on to the train again to check out the other branch of this northern reach of the Metropolitan Line, the route to Amersham.

Everywhere I went in the suburbs of north London, I was impressed by the quality of housing and by the amount of it. Glasgow has its discreet, leafy suburbs, but they are small and few. London has dozens and dozens of them, emphasising the depth of prosperity in this part of the country.

The quality of the commuter cars in the station car park at Moor Park suggested that it would be the classiest yet. The streets were lined with mature trees. Some of the roads were not even public highways. A sign on Main Avenue informed the public that it had 'not been dedicated as a highway'. This announcement was by a company, Moor Park (1958) Ltd. You can't get more exclusive than that. Somehow Drumchapel Opportunities or the Craigmillar Initiative don't have the same ring of quality.

You can also tell the quality of an area by its shops. Here, there was a very upmarket Chinese restaurant, the Peking Garden, and 14 very classy shops, including one selling local paintings. It didn't seem like the centre of anything, so I asked a young passer-by if these were all the shops in Moor Park. 'Yes,' she said, tongue in cheek, 'it's really exciting round here.'

I had only stopped at Moor Park because it was the first chance to change to the Amersham branch. But it was worth seeing. I added it to my growing list of places in London where I would be prepared to stay. On the stairway of the station was an advertisement for the Moor Park Metropolitan Football Team. The manager, Bob Birrell, was looking for games against teams 'both old or young, of either sex'. Bob had given his phone number on the ad. So I used it. He told me that he had been with the Underground for over 20 years and was now in middle management as a duty station manager, reporting to a group station manager. Bob has between 12 and 24 stations and at least 16 staff under him. Aware of his responsibility to the community, he had the idea of using the empty wall space at stations to build relationships with the local schools. Out of his budget, he provided frames at ten stations and the schools now regularly submit paintings and drawings which are displayed there. Most of them were the usual rubbish that kids draw – not quite as amateurish as Miro, but getting that way. But it was quite clear that they had enjoyed doing it.

'I love the thrill they get when they show their mums and dads their own work hanging there beside the professionally designed posters,' Bob added.

As to the football and the generous non-sexist nature of his ad . . .

'It's not so much that,' he explained, 'It's more that my team is so past it now, and so desperate for games, that we'd even play against women.'

A dash of realism to throw in the face of the politically correct Nineties. Women can't play football. Yes, there was a league set-up, sponsored by Provident Mutual, and each line had two teams – one at each end. They also played against disreputable outsiders like taxi drivers and sixth formers – but not from Harrow.

I got on to the train and travelled to another of Bob's stations, Chorleywood. Before the station, the line runs under a low bridge carrying the infamous M25 and, coming into Chorleywood station itself, the line is elevated, giving a good view of a neat village and the Sportsman's Hotel. I rather liked the sound of that.

This branch ends at Amersham, which is the most westerly point on the London Underground, 27 miles from Oxford Circus. Amersham Town Council has the smallest municipal office I have ever been in. It occupies four rooms, upstairs in a two-storey building in the High Street, above a firm of architects.

Amersham is a classic old settlement mentioned in the Doomsday Book, going back to the Romans and even to the Bronze Age – a settlement of that vintage had been unearthed as a by-product of roadworks in 1987. A real blessing to archaeologists, these modern motorways. How many treasures would have remained hidden from scientific scrutiny and analysis if it had not been for the roads lobby and their friends in the Department of Transport?

I also spotted a black Hillman Imp with a K registration – that is a K at the *end* of the number, denoting 1972. Hillman Imps were, of course, only built at Linwood, near Glasgow. My wife had one. The water pump had to be replaced six times. The factory is now shut.

On the train waiting to leave, a very un-Amersham scene occurred. It was enacted between two dirty, unkempt hippies. She came on to the train with me. Dressed in stripey pyjama bottoms and a woven grey top that was neither a shirt nor a jacket, she sat with her spotty face and a brass knob through one nostril. He appeared at the door with *his* pyjama bottoms of different stripes, a not-quite-kaftan top, dreadlocks dyed orange at the ends, and a dirty face.

He called her over to say goodbye. This he did by trying to smother her with hugs and kisses. Her body language should have been discouraging. For the whole of the 15 minutes that this went on, she stood sideways to him, her shoulder in his chest, responding to his attempts with pecks on the cheek – the way women do who are not the least interested in the sexual implications of the contact, but who do not want entirely to discourage the attention. There was not going to be much free love here.

It sounded like she was leaving on a journey much longer than mine.

'When will you be back?' he asked, longingly. 'Eight o'clock?'

'Oh no,' she said. 'It could be much later than that.'

'I'll wait for you,' he promised.

67

This pledge caused her to show the desperation for the train to leave that I was sharing. But it wouldn't leave. So she responded to his promise by talking about typing speeds. Some hippy! The train made a sound to go, he jumped off and she made her way back to her seat. But it was a false alarm and he came back on again. She had to go back to the door for another session. He tried to hold her hand. She took one of his hands in both of hers and patted it urgently, mirroring the rhythm of the train that she hoped was leaving. It's great to have read Desmond Morris's *Manwatching*. You get so much more out of travel.

There was now only one part of the Metropolitan Line left to explore – the other western branch which ends at Uxbridge. To do this I had to retrace my steps to Harrow-on-the-Hill.

On the way back west again, at West Harrow, I was joined by a couple of Underground employees with scythes, a cameo which added a quaint, rural, anachronistic atmosphere to the journey. Old and new technologies mingle more or less comfortably in third world countries, and even in Eastern Europe. But it was weird here. Their task soon became clear because, after Ruislip, we were out in the country and the side of the track was overgrown with grass and weeds. What more appropriate technology could there be for this job than men with scythes?

Hillingdon station is stunningly modern, all white tubing and glass. Very much in keeping with the Underground tradition of using contemporary architecture at all stages of its development. The result is a jumble of styles as you go from one part of the system to the next. This could be discomfiting but, once you get used to it, it can help you to identify different eras – and, I suppose, the history of architecture and building materials. If only they would keep older stations as clean as they do newer ones like Hillingdon.

We then ran downhill into Uxbridge station, which was a classic of a different type. It seemed to me of Sixties concrete, which was relieved by the only stained-glass windows I had noticed on the Tube.

Although there is no historical evidence of a village at Uxbridge before the end of the twelfth century, a Stone Age hunters' campsite has been discovered relatively recently. Locals claim it is the most important in Britain. Naturally.

But Uxbridge was a town for farmers and traders rather than hunter-gatherers and built its success first on its market and secondly on its location on a main road. By the early 1800s the town was the staging post for journeys to and from London and Oxford, Bristol, Hereford, Worcester and all points west.

I don't know what images 'stagecoach' conjures up for you. Me? Apart from John Wayne and the Western variety, I've seen them on Christmas cards, in films of Dickens' novels and when highwaymen hold them up as they lurch apprehensively along deserted rural roads in costume dramas.

On the other hand, my knowledge of railways comes from books. I have studied a lot of economic history, from A-level to two years at university. Despite knowing all of the facts – at least enough to pass the exams comfortably – I now realise that I acquired a completely distorted view of the great railway age. I always looked on rail travel as rather like the Sony Walkman – the kind of invention that nobody knew that they wanted until the market and slick advertising taught them to use it in all sorts of annoying ways.

I had imagined thousands of people in their hamlets and villages sitting around with no thought, much less desire, to travel to the next town. I had imagined the scene as George Stephenson, busy adapting one of Scotland's many inventions, had thought that he could persuade sceptical investors to part with their cash by promising: 'Yes, it will take you from Stockton to Darlington *and back*!'

Then, eventually, the Great Eastern, or Western, comes along and lays a track into town, rather like a cable television company today. Apart from the NIMBY objectors, no one pays any attention for a few days, or even weeks. Then out of curiosity, or boredom, some people try it out. And suddenly trains become very popular indeed as a form of leisure experience.

When I discovered that 80 stagecoaches poured into Uxbridge *every day* I realised what a misconception this was. Far from being a docile, indolent, immobile lot, the population of nineteenth-century Britain had obviously all sorts of urgent reasons to travel. Because the stagecoach was not comfortable. It was cramped. It was crowded. It was cold. And it was slow. At the beginning of the nineteenth century, the journey from London to Oxford took all day, with frequent stops. If you wanted to travel to Edinburgh from the English capital you had to reckon on a journey of ten days.

All this travelling generated a huge infrastructure. There were 500 vehicles a day passing along the busiest roads. In 1825 there were 25 coaches a day running between Chelsea and London alone, much to the disgust of Chelsea residents who had moved out of the city to this little village for peace and quiet. But if we concentrate on Uxbridge's 80, and reckon on four horses per coach (and often there were six), then you had 320 horses coming into Uxbridge every day, each one having to be fed and watered. The passengers, six, eight or ten per coach plus the coachdrivers, also needed feeding and watering. Uxbridge had 54 inns – and several breweries – to cater for them!

The railway therefore filled a real need. And it is not surprising that, with its undreamed-of speed, it soon networked the country and generated economic growth.

I walked out into Uxbridge's quaintish pedestrianised main street with its Tudor-style shop fronts. I was visiting these places mid-morning or mid-afternoon in the middle of the week. Yet all of the shopping streets were busy. It was not so much the bustle of people rushing round doing the messages (Glaswegian for making the necessary everyday purchases of things like milk and bread). Rather, it was the unhurried wandering of the leisure shopper. This surely denotes a huge social change. Is it unemployment, shift patterns, an ageing population or something else that gives so many people the spare time to wander around shops in the middle of the afternoon?

But I hadn't time to join them. I had completed my task on this line, but there were plenty more to explore. So, without more ado, it was back into the welcoming arms of the station – literally, for that is part of its design.

CHAPTER FOUR

TRAFALGAR SQUARED

The Jubilee, the newest of the London Underground tentacles, is only really a separate line north of Baker Street, or even Finchley Road. This was originally one branch of the Bakerloo Line, leading to Stanmore.

South of Baker Street, it merely parallels the existing Bakerloo Line in a section of new twin tunnels terminating at what is now called Charing Cross. But when the planned extension is completed – and that could take until 1998 – an entirely new area will be opened up to Tube passengers through London's redeveloped Docklands.

Anyone like me, whose knowledge of London's geography has been dominated by the Underground map for more than 40 years, is likely to be in a state of confusion about Charing Cross. Its precise whereabouts seems to be a matter of some doubt, for it keeps moving. On the surface, Charing Cross is tangible enough. It is, after all, one of the four stations on the Monopoly board. But underground, it moves around mysteriously.

The first Charing Cross beneath the streets was the one on the District Line, opened on 30 May 1870. Then the Bakerloo Line, thrusting southwards in 1906, and stopping off at Trafalgar Square, reached the Thames at a deep level station which it called Embankment, which was more or less directly underneath the District Line's Charing Cross. Meanwhile, the Northern Line got in on the act with its own station called Charing Cross a few hundred yards to the north, deep under the mainline station: it opened in June 1907. But when the Northern was extended southwards in 1914, its former Charing Cross station was renamed Charing Cross (Strand), and its new terminus, even closer to the District Line Charing Cross, was christened Charing Cross (Embankment), and was linked in linked in with the Bakerloo Line, which changed its name to suit. A year later, on 9 May 1915, all three became Charing Cross, while Charing Cross (Strand) became just Strand. Are you following this?

Strand was closed by London Transport on 16 June 1973 – but only temporarily, because someone, somewhere, had a master plan. In 1974, Charing Cross (that's the one now interchanging on all three lines) reverted to one of its former names, but without the brackets, Charing Cross Embankment. This was but a stepping stone to a further reincarnation two years later, when it became simply Embankment. And this allowed the completion of the grand plan in 1979, when the Jubilee line arrived on the scene at Trafalgar Square. At this point, Trafalgar Square, one of the most famous of all London landmarks, disappeared completely from the face of the Underground map. Without moving a muscle, on 1 May, it had transformed itself magically, boasting a new subterranean interchange with the former Strand or Charing Cross (Strand) station to become what it had been originally called on the Northern Line in 1907 – Charing Cross! Now you know. But please don't ask the way to Trafalgar Square. It doesn't exist any more. At least in the Underground's universe.

But – back in that parallel existence called reality – Trafalgar Square is, in fact, the biggest of all the capital's war memorials. Unlike the others, and particularly the stark Cenotaph in Whitehall, this does not mourn the loss of good and brave men. It celebrates the triumph over Napoleon. Nelson's column still sticks one finger up at the French. A triumph for the democratic style of town planning over the autocratic grandeur of Haussman's Paris, some would argue. But not that democratic. The fountains were built to break up the public space and the hostile crowds that the government feared might gather.

These fountains may have done that in the nineteenth century. In the twentieth, they used to assist generations of Scottish football fans, in London for the biennial clash with the Auld Enemy, to exercise their democratic right to do themselves severe injury by jumping from their 20-foot height into six inches of dirty water. Indeed, it was incidents such as the death of one fan who did exactly that which led to the abandonment of the fixture.

There used to be a Lyons' Corner House at the Charing Cross

side of Trafalgar Square – with a Scottish connection. This particular Corner House was famous for its rook pie. All of Lyons's establishments may well have been famous for this delicacy, I do not know. The story relates to this one. Every week from Brechin, a sleepy little town in the north east of Scotland, a box of dead rooks would be loaded on to the Aberdeen train. There it would be transferred to the night sleeper to London. The next day the box would be delivered to the Corner House in Trafalgar Square, the rooks unloaded and the few pounds that they cost pinned to the inside of the box which then made its way back to Brechin for next week's load.

I discovered a far better place to eat. Fat Boys, plonked down in a gap site in Maiden Lane, is straight out of a 1950s Captain Marvel comic. It is an all-American Diner, a metal tube with shaded windows cut in the side. It has those wee round button seats on single metal legs bolted to the floor along the whole length of the counter. I discovered a similar treasure near Liverpool Street Station. This one was Diner Number 849, the last one to be manufactured. Dating back to 1955 it had been built in Worcester, Massachusetts. Now re-sited in London, it serves cholesterol. Lots and lots of it. It also carried its own language on the menu, with English translation. An *eskimo highball* was water, *cow paste*, butter and *whistlers*, beans.

Charing Cross is only the temporary end of the Jubilee Line, for a vast extension is under construction which will take the line past London Bridge, through Docklands and Canary Wharf and ending up at Stratford.

The cost will run to billions. Money well spent, I say. And London Underground has provided an economic model to prove it. This shows the value of the social and economic benefits that result from the Underground services. These benefits are calculated by comparing those arising from the Tube services with a hypothetical situation where there is no Underground.

There are three categories of benefits. In the first are those benefits that are felt directly by passengers and which are generated because, despite the moans that are the right of every London commuter, the services of the Underground are more valued by the customer than the price that they have to pay. In other words, if the fares went up, most travellers would still pay them.

Secondly, there are the benefits from reduced surface congestion. These are the value of the savings in journey time, pollution and the reduced risk of accidents as a result of traffic diverted from the roads to the Underground.

In 1995 these two categories of benefits are together said to have amounted to £1,279 million.

The third group of benefits are the benefits to the UK economy of 'knock-on' economic effects. These are measured by a model–based calculation of the scale of reduction in economic activity that would result from the absence of the Underground. These benefits have been calculated at £2,013 million.

Thus the total benefit of £3,293 million can be set against the total economic cost of providing the Underground of £789 million. So society is better off to the tune of £2,504 million. And that's every year.

If the very mention of economics has given you a sore head and you're trying to skip to the next bit, start here.

What all that means is that the Underground is great value for money.

The Jubilee Line was named to commemorate the silver anniversary, in 1977, of the Queen's accession to the throne. Its opening by Prince Charles on 1 May 1979 recalled the fact that a previous Prince of Wales opened the world's first electric tube railway, the City and South London in 1890, which is now part of the Northern Line.

The Jubilee route north is a natural one in that it complements the routes to the suburbs of the Metropolitan Line on the one hand (the left, looking at that familiar London Underground map) and the Northern on the other.

It was therefore sensible to begin at Baker Street and from there to explore the unique part of the Jubilee Line.

St John's Wood, the station for Lord's, was an essential stop. But I could not cram a visit to the temple of English culture into such a busy day. And, anyway, it was one place that I wanted to see living its role. I made special plans to visit it on a Test match day.

Especially as it was the cricket that hastened the development of this section of the Tube, although then i was the first part of the

ssmen to have quick access behind the opening of the s accessed from the station lf part of the Jubilee Line. the capital T) and reckoned st Indies would be a perfect l the whole of the five-day hich day to go. The last day ould be the last day? Given ould be lost in three or four the event I decided to take r the weather and opted for

n at the station that morning eople who didn't fancy the ravel on to the next station s. This standard of service be included in a day ticket

ground, but it is a pleasant suburb on the City's rim'. -tall, expensive, apartment were hard at work. It must here there is a demand for e were tee-shirts with the front. And I was offered a reppes. The market testing it again. he home of English cricket, n and the Taverners' Bar by

made a point of recording in words or on video how special was the first day's atmosphere at Lord's. I could feel it immediately. The stands were full, the weather was hot – and the grass, on which I was able to walk even although the start of play was only an hour away, was green and smooth.

But the thing which makes any sporting event special is that everyone takes it seriously. Those not interested in sport often sneer at its triviality. 'Twenty-two grown men chasing a ball' is how they refer to football. And, depending on your values, you might classify sport as relatively unimportant, although millions would disagree.

Attending an international event in a sport that was not mine, I almost managed to sit outside the atmosphere and consider this. Cricket is a game, and you can have good fun playing it, irrespective of the result, if you are just treating it as a bit of fun.

But these players weren't having fun, at least not that kind of fun. This was dead serious. The opening batsmen walked out aware of the expectations of the home crowd. Aware of the necessity to succeed, they weren't about to relax and enjoy themselves.

I had managed to talk my way into the press box and, as the day progressed, I found the activity there as fascinating as the play. I was shown to my seat by an Irish steward in a green jacket.

'I like the jacket,' I told him.

'Pure polyester,' he replied. 'It'll be off in 15 minutes.'

A freelance representing *The Guardian* wandered in looking for the seat that corresponded to his ticket number.

'You can forget about numbers here,' he was told by the fat hack sitting in his seat.

'Come and join the Illingworth fan club in the second row,' shouted another.

'There's the Illingworth fan club and the Atherton fan club. Which one do you want?'

None of this diverted the third reporter who was using a pal's phone to ring his own mobile which was sitting in front of him. He stared at it contentedly.

The 'fan club' jibe was a reference to a story in that morning's *Sun* about a fall-out between manager and captain over the selection and then the omission of wicket-keeper Rhodes. The *Mirror* man, who had been scooped, was desperately debunking the story to anyone who would listen. But, as the umpires took the field, Illingworth popped up on the telly to put his case. All the hacks, led by the man from the *Mirror*, abandoned their seats to crowd round the box and scribble down every word. No wonder the newspaper boys hate the telly. Here were people getting the information direct from one of the principals, without the filter paper of the press. Such is the dislike of these two groups of media persons, that, in my capacity of public relations consultant (my day job), I have run a press conference where the newspaper reporters refused to sit in the seats allocated to them because the TV people would use them as 'camera fodder'. Rather, they sat huddled at the back of the room and called the sports personality over to them after the cameras had stopped turning.

The same telly can distort, though. For one thing you get no idea of how tall the West Indian bowlers really are.

The press box is an even better place than the famous stand from which to watch the game. At 12.15 it was time for drinks – for the hacks, not the players. Attractive PR persons – (why do I call them persons? There were no men.) – handed out wine, courtesy of Cornhill Insurance. Many people enjoyed two or three glasses.

You are certainly well looked after. Apart from the hospitality, you get supplied with a match programme, statistics of all the current players' records, world records, results of all matches between the two teams and so on. You also get a page of betting odds, and a couple of stories written for you. Like 'Atherton's turn to Join Lord's Test Century Club' and 'Series Statistics Indicate Uphill Battle'.

At lunch – free ('Cornhill will be serving a buffet lunch, with wine and soft drinks, in the press bar on the first three days of the match. Sandwiches will be available for purchase on the remaining days of play.') – I took the opportunity to wander around the rest of the ground. In the cricket museum is a moving memorial to the dead of two world wars, 'secure from change in their light-hearted way'. The memorial is dedicated to 'cricketers of all lands who gave their life in the cause of freedom'. There must be no other sport that is played only by the good guys.

The Ashes are kept permanently here, as is the sparrow permanently bowled out by Jehangir Khan in 1936.

In the afternoon, E.W. Swanton came into the press box. 'Much better, so far,' he commented to me. 'If we get 300, it'll be a game.' But everyone was saying that.

I thought I had better take this opportunity to interview him. He had seen 300 or more Test matches – 'Not as many as Johnny Woodcock. He writes better than anyone'.

I had noticed that there seemed to be no opposition supporters at all in the ground. I thought that he might know why. 'The cost of the tickets is one thing. They are made to feel unwelcome. They are exuberant, they like to shout and sing and dance and the authorities here discouraged them.' Typical English attitude, 'none of this enjoying yourselves'. The West Indians fans now go to the Oval where the atmosphere is much more relaxed.

As I left him, one of the other journalists began biting his ear trying to persuade him to write a piece for Ramadhin and Valentine's testimonial programme. 'You'll be in good company. John Major is writing the foreword.'

Ramadhin he came up to bowl
Bowled the ball right up Cowdrey's hole
Cowdrey said, 'Oh, my bum!'
Valentine said, 'Fie, Fie, Fum.'

was the calypso that I remembered from the Fifties. It wouldn't be in good company with John Major, so I didn't offer it for inclusion.

Back at the cricket, 50p changed hands when Smith got his 50. When he was in his forties, there had been a discussion over the number of chances he had given. Two? Three? The man from the Press Association arbitrated. Two. They all agreed.

As the score moved on, one asked 'Who's silly Illy now?'

Then the male correspondent from Pakistan started taking photographs of the female correspondent from the *Independent*.

Jeff Powell from the *Daily Mail* writes in longhand, which is maybe why he does it so well. Another scribe complains that his wireless batteries have run out. A third announces that he has to let his phone battery run down completely before he can recharge it. 'Where is the cricket writers' dinner this year?' asks a fourth.

The press box applaud the 100 partnership. 'Too early,' shouts Wendy Wimbush. The men argue with her, but she is right. 'They've marked two, not one, for two no-balls,' she explains. This is the first time that I realised that there are different scoring systems for different classes of game. How odd.

Another diversion developed. The telly was showing the third place play-off game in the Rugby World Cup, England versus France. The French kicker misses. 'Who bunged him, then,' asks a hack.

Woodcock is too busy blethering to watch the game and misses Smith's dismissal. But after he has been put right by three or four people, he mutters repeatedly, 'Fancy getting out to Hooper.' I am the only one listening to him.

On the telly, France score. 'That's means we have to pre–qualify for the next World Cup,' shouts one. 'Does that mean trips?' asks another.

A rumour that Major has resigned as Prime Minister sweeps the box. It is clear from the confused discussion that the hacks don't understand the political system any better than they do the scoring at Test matches. But will he still be asked to write the foreword? As the talk rages on, incoherently, one asks from his word processor, as he inserts his unique view of the match: 'Was that Atherton toss win his first in six or eight?'

I left a few minutes before stumps. I was surprised that not more were joining me. I had always thought of cricket as a game you drift into and out of. But the ground was still packed as I was leaving.

On the way out across by the Nursery end (it really was a plant nursery, not a breeding ground for young cricketers), there was a queue of people trying to get in. On closer inspection, they were all men, and poorly dressed men at that. In senior football, there used to be a tradition of opening the gates about 20 minutes from the end of the match and allowing small boys and the unemployed in for nothing to see the end of the game. Was this a similar tradition?

But when I looked even more closely I saw that most of these men had the appearance of down-and-outs being checked in. I knew I should have gone across to question them. But they looked so miserable as they offered their names to a girl holding a clip-board that I decided to postpone my enquiry.

The new assistant secretary to the MCC told me the story. They were what they appeared to be, casual labourers looking for work. At the end of play on big match days, Lord's recruits between 120 and 180 'temporary groundsmen' to tidy the place up for the next day. The tradition goes back as far as the current ground administrator can remember.

And I was right not to enquire at the time. As most of the men are in receipt of a state benefit of one kind or another, they do not welcome snoopers. But the snoopers, or at least their colleagues, were still inside enjoying the free drink.

As I said, the Lord's visit was a special treat. My exploration of the Jubilee Line really started at Swiss Cottage. The Swiss cottage isn't a cottage at all. In fact, I don't think they're even called cottages in Switzerland. It's supposed to be a chalet. And it certainly has some chalet-like features. It appears to be made of wood. It has a balcony. And flower boxes. But the flowers are not geraniums. And the colours wrapped round the columns are the Italian national ones, not the red and white of the Swiss. Inside, the bars are big and comfortable with an atmosphere more club-like than après-ski.

Evidently, it was opened in 1840 after the English had a brief love affair with Swiss architecture. The Prince Consort had a chalet built in Osborne on the Isle of Wight and Swiss Cottage copied it. I hope it's a poor copy. Prince Albert usually got things right. Still, it's good fun to see such an out-of-place feature in the middle of a big city.

But I was here to look for something of much greater significance – the Freud Museum. I walked up College Crescent past an intriguingly well-proportioned drinking fountain, covered with a little roof. I was sorry that it was not working, but was being used by a flower seller to store his bits and pieces. It was erected by friends of Samuel Palmer of North Tower. They must have thought a lot of him.

Freud stayed at 20 Maresfield Gardens from 1938 until his death the next year. He picked a nice place to live. The house is big, three storeys, a lot of windows facing the front with a number of them filled with tall plants.

What could this house tell me about Freud? On the inside of one window, I could see a closed grille like the doors of an old-fashioned lift. Was this a sign of his insecurity? The blinds were drawn in another room. Significant?

The front door was closed, but a small sign indicated 'Open. Please walk in'. I suddenly felt the analysis switching from Freud to me. Was this a test? Behind the desk a young, blonde girl was

80

chewing gum. I asked her the cost of admission. She didn't answer directly. Instead she told me that it was too near to closing time to start a tour. I turned away, wondering whether I was expected to be more assertive. As I opened the door to leave, I noticed a tiny sign on an antique box. It was too small to read, so I picked it up to discover what the great man had used this for. 'Please do not sit on trunk.' I'd failed another test.

I left and walked back down Maresfield Gardens, desperately aware of the lines between the paving stones, and conscious that I must not try to walk on them – or display any paranoia in trying *not* to walk on them. I managed it, and got safely back to the station.

I'm not really a fan of burial grounds, but I thought that Hampstead Cemetery might somehow be more upmarket than most. It's a ten–minute walk from Finchley Road, slightly less from West Hampstead, heading northwards towards Cricklewood along lissom suburban streets. You can judge for yourself if the following collection of immortal gravestones constitutes a class above the rest: horn-player Dennis Brain; actresses Marie Lloyd and Dame Gladys Cooper; Sebastian de Ferranti, 'inventor'; and Joseph Lister, the pioneer of antiseptic surgery. There's also one Horace Short, whose dramatic life included being captured by cannibals in the South Sea islands. He must have been pretty unpalatable to them, however, because they decided instead to worship him as their king. It must have been a year of plenty for the South Sea islands.

Neasden is one of those districts of London which people like to sneer at. It was once voted 'the most uncharismatic place in England'. I have my doubts. Have those voters ever been to parts of Liverpool, Stockton or even large swatches of the A1 through rural Yorkshire? Or Carlisle? Nevertheless, Neasden must be a noisy place in which to live. The station itself is perched on top of a hill just beside a large Underground train depot. And I wonder if you can hear the roar from Wembley Stadium, just a mile or two away, over the cacophony of the North Circular Road, which encloses Neasden's northern and western territorial flanks?

But Neasden now has something unique in England, which might just give it the wow factor: its own Hindu temple. Not some converted suburban villa or even a country house with its own grounds. This is the genuine all–marble effort, trying hard to compete with the Taj Mahal itself, if you'll excuse the mixed religions.

Not that it is easy to find from the Tube. Many people must have been before me. But the crudely-drawn map on the temporary notice-board is not much help. For one thing the scale is lacking, so you have no idea how far it would be to walk. I left the station, walked downhill looking for the promised roundabout which, according to the map, was about two feet away. Three hundred yards later, I turned back to ask the man in the station shop exactly how to get there. A girl in one of those Peruvian or Tibetan patterned jackets was asking the same questions. He got exasperated as we pressed him for directions. I guessed from his Pakistani accent that he was probably a Muslim, so would not be best pleased with all the attention that the Hindus were attracting. The girl was going to walk. I got some reassurance that I had been heading in the right direction and went off again to catch the bus to Tesco's that apparently would lead me to the temple. It was a long walk to the bus stop. And a long wait for the bus.

As I waited, the girl arrived. The shopkeeper had convinced her that it was too far to walk, so she was getting the bus, too. To kill time until the Number 16 arrived, I asked her about herself. Taking a stab at her accent, I guessed she was Spanish. 'No,' she said, 'I'm from Argentina,' in a way that suggested that I'd guessed Mongolian or Samoan. Her father ran a farm and she was in London attending a training course at Kew Gardens. I told her that I was writing a book about London and that now she was in it.

I therefore needed her name and her age. She was 22, which I wrote down carefully. But when she claimed that she was called Cynthia Taylor, I burst out laughing. It was true, she assured me, her grandfather or 'somebody' had been English. She was from Corrientes.

Had I been to Argentina she asked?

'No,' I had to confess, adding, ingratiatingly, 'but I've seen it from Brazil.'

That went down as well as the guess about Spanish. In my embarrassment, if she had asked, I would have handed her back the Falklands.

We got on the bus, and off again at Tesco's, which appeared to have changed its name to IKEA, but nobody called it that. That wasn't the end of the journey. The driver told us that we would have to take yet another bus. Then a woman passenger convinced us that it was near enough to walk. But the directions still weren't clear. So I stopped the first person we met as we stumbled about Brentfield Road. She turned out to be a Scot who lived just round the corner. The temple was two minutes away. She hadn't bothered to visit it, and was astonished that I had come down from Glasgow to see it.

It *was* two minutes away. And it *is* magnificent.

It was the biggest surprise I had in London to see it at the end of the road. It looks so out of place. But set in spacious, sculptured grounds, its appearance transports you to the East and it's the rest of the street that begins to look out of place. Maybe it's the gleaming white stone. Maybe it is the innumerable oriental towers. Maybe it's the hundreds of voluntary helpers – because, just like in India, there are dozens of people anxious to advise you, help you, guide you, get in your way.

Peering through the black metal gates, I said goodbye to Cynthia, telling her that I would leave her to enjoy the spectacle by herself. 'It is better,' she said.

Just a few weeks later, the Neasden Hindu temple hit the national headlines, as a frenzy of excitement reverberated round the world at news that statues of the Hindu elephant–god Ganesh were said to be sipping milk from proffered spoons. Apparently North London dairies did a roaring trade.

I walked across the broad courtyard to have a look at the carved white stone. Then upstairs and on to the polished wooden floors to deposit my shoes in Shoe Rack No. 2. I joined the flow and walked through the ante-rooms, upstairs and on to the white marble floor of the temple itself. All along the way helpers held up handwritten signs asking for silence. At the entrance to the temple proper, the queue was divided into men and women. The women's queue moved faster. Workmen were still developing the intricate detail on the carved marble. There were little side altars with carved wooden doors lying open, to show doll-like statues of the gods and goddesses clothed in garish colours, with their names underneath. One god's altar was piled so high with bananas that his name was obscured. Milk and bananas – an odd combination of sacrificial foods.

I came back to put my shoes on again. They were still hot. It must have been a short tour.

Then came the long journey back to the Tube station. I walked back to Tesco's for the Number 16. Just across from the bus stop is a modest brick-built Catholic chapel, which contrasted sharply with the opulence of the temple. It's not often that you see the Church of Rome upstaged.

The bus took a long route back to Neasden Parade, slipping on and off the North Circular Road until I was sure that both the driver and I were lost. But together we made it. Walking back to the station, I discovered that the roundabout had a museum on it, the Grange Museum of Local History. Thank God, it was shut and I could avoid it without feeling guilty. The local history of Neasden was not something that I felt I could handle at that moment.

As I joined the train again at Wembley Park, my feet were on their last legs. I planned a quick look at Stanmore, and then back to base camp to write up my notes. What fascinated me about Stanmore was the huge complex of government offices shown on the map. They looked as if they could and did employ thousands, just the sort of jobs that could be dispersed to the periphery of the kingdom. Surely, after the earlier disappointment of Mahatma Gandhi House, they would at least belong to the Ministry of Defence, even if not part of our germ warfare initiative (which doesn't, of course, exist).

I walked out into the bright sunlight at Stanmore, not knowing that I was in the middle of a record–breaking summer and so marvelling yet again at the wonderful southern climate. I picked my way gingerly across London Road and sat down at the bus stop to plan my attack. Across the road, buses lined up outside the station to collect the arriving commuters. Spouses of both sexes sat in cars for the same purpose.

Estimating the distance on the map to the government offices, I decided that I could just about hobble it, when something even more interesting caught my eye. The government offices were on Brockley Hill, a long, straight road. What I noticed was written sideways along the road on the map – the words 'Watling Street (Roman Road)'.

I had heard all about Watling Street in my Latin classes. Well, I had heard that it was one of England's Roman roads. But I had always wanted to ask a question, but didn't dare. I went to school in the 1950s, a time when you got the 'belt' for asking cheeky questions. The 'belt' or 'tawse' was the instrument of punishment in Scottish schools. Three or four feet long and two or three inches wide, the most fearsome of these leather straps was the Lochgelly, after the village in Fife where they were produced. Sadistic teachers, i.e. most of them, used to hang their belts over their shoulders as they paraded about the classroom looking for people to punish. Indiscipline, impertinence or ignorance were rewarded by between one and six strokes on the palms of the outstreched hands. The wealds could last for days.

So you had to be very, very careful about the kind of questions you asked. Cheeky questions fell into two categories. First, there were questions which had no strict connection with the subject under discussion – there was no inter-disciplinary approach back then. And then there were questions which the teacher could not answer, the height of impertinence. The question that I had in mind fell into both categories at once (and remember I was 13 at the time). It was: 'How could Watling Street, with its distinctive English ending, possibly be the name of a Roman road, when all the Latin endings we were forced to learn were -us or -um or -a?'

I had to wait until now for my answer. Watling Street does not come from Latin, but from the name of a Saxon leader, Waecel, whose people were know as Waeclingas.

Anyway, I wanted to see it and to walk it. To add to the interest, the map indicated the site of a Roman camp at the top of the hill opposite the Royal Orthopaedic Hospital. But I was never going to be able to get that far in my state.

A car stopped. 'Can you tell me where Honeypot Lane is?' the driver asked, with the unerring instinct drivers have for picking out strangers. But I was better equipped than most strangers. 'Haven't a clue, but I'll look at my map.' Together we found it, and then I persuaded him to give me a lift to the bottom of Brockley Hill, even although it was in the opposite direction.

I thought I was more than halfway there, but I was still miles away. Again there was evidence of prosperity, with more beautiful houses tucked in just off the road. Not only were the houses mock Tudor, the garages were as well. One even had a fox-shaped weather vane.

The government offices were a series of low-rise huts surrounded by a high fence. The entrance was well off the road and, although I could see a commissionaire, there were no signs indicating what was going on in there. I had to wait until later to check. I then found that they were indeed the offices of some part of the Ministry of Defence, employing 3,000 people. Further information was difficult to extract.

I walked on up the hill. Roman roads may be straight, though this one wasn't as straight as all that. Maybe the legionnaires succumbed to motorway fatigue if they were *too* straight. These were the kind of ramblings I was indulging in to try and keep my mind off my feet and my knee. I wondered if they had an out-patient department of the Royal Orthopaedic Hospital. And I wondered if, under Thatcher's health service, they would treat me this far from home without demanding payment.

I was looking forward to seeing the English at play on the local tennis courts. But this part of the green belt was being improved by Wimpey (the builders, that is, not the burger chain). I had now run out of things to look at, and I still wasn't halfway up the hill.

Pear Wood, with its fish pond, was on my left off Watling Street, but I had difficulty seeing it through a screen of trees. The ground inside had been built up by about six feet, so all that you could look into was an embankment. At last I got to Wood Lane, dodged the traffic across the road, and looked into the Roman Camp.

As with most Roman camps there was not much to see, just a green field. But there was a little blue plaque identifying this as the site of a Roman pottery circa AD 65–160. Very late, considering that every schoolboy knows that Julius Caesar landed in Britain in 55 BC. What is often forgotten is that, although he left rather smartly for his little local difficulty with Brutus, his pals who came in earnest, some 90 years later, in AD 43, stayed on for a bit longer. They were here until AD 409 in fact. Twice as long as the British domination of India.

It is not true to say that the Romans founded London. There had been a Celtic fort at a bend in the Wallbrook stream where it overlooked the Thames tidal lake. This location might or might not have had the name Llyn-Din, the lake fort. It's a neat explanation, but philologically debatable. According to experts in Celtic usage, an adjective or other qualifying word should follow, not precede, the main noun, in the annoying way that French sometimes still does. As schoolboys, we had hours of endless fun in the French class repeatedly asking each other the difference between 'mon propre trou' and 'mon trou propre'. So, 'lake fort' would be, in Celtic, the other way round ,'fort lake' or Din-Llyn.

And so 'London' should really be 'Donlon': 'Maybe it's because I'm a Donloner . . .' 'Donlon Bridge is falling down . . .' Doesn't work, does it?

While the Romans never did locate their settlements on British sites, they did build a military station opposite the British one in the autumn of AD 43 and they Latinised the name to Donlonium –sorry, Londinium.

It was at first merely a Roman fort, located exactly at Cannon Street station, from where the first London bridge crossed the Thames. The fort was just beginning to develop commercially, bringing a degree of prosperity and a bit of culture to the area, when Boadicea – the archetypal Essex woman, the Margaret Thatcher of the early Britons – burnt it down in AD 60. OK, she was from East Anglia, but that's near enough for me.

London must be one of the most flammable of all cities in history, because – as well as the Great Fire that we all know about, and Boadicea's less great, less publicised but just as effective conflagration – it burnt down again in around AD 130 in the 'Hadrianic Fire'. This must have been the wall man, on his way back from the north, perhaps?

In between times, London boomed as a trading centre, became the capital of the province and could boast in its newly–built basilica the longest Roman building outside latter Italy (a term that is, I believe, used by scholars as the opposite of terms like former Yugoslavia).

No one is very sure when the London wall was built – AD 200 is mentioned by some scholars – but all agree that it was 3¼ miles in circumference, enclosing a space of about 380 acres.

The site that I identified near Stanmore turned out to be Sulloniacae, the first 'posting station' on the northern part of Watling Street. Its location was deliberately chosen at the top of the hill that I had just slogged up, because of the views it commanded. I bet the legionnaires appreciated that as much as I did. These posting stations began as small forts to guard the roads and impress the local barbarians with the might of the Roman Empire. But villages quickly grew up around them. In Sulloniacae's case, the presence of clay led to the establishment of a pottery to supply local needs. As the prosperity and population of London diminished, the pottery faced a declining market and closed around AD 160.

I staggered a few yards further up the hill to a welcome bus stop and collapsed on to the bench.

The banner strung along the hospital palings reminded me of how bad my knee might become if I didn't get it looked after. It was advertising the Great Hip and Knee Walk for the Wishbone Trust. All the walkers would have replacement joints. It sounded like a self-perpetuating activity. Wouldn't it just give rise to a need for more of the same scarce facilities that the charitable effort was designed to overcome?

As I waited, I was joined by a companion with a name badge. He obviously worked in the hospital. Perhaps I could get some informal advice on my knee.

I started obliquely. 'I just came up to look at the Roman camp.'

'What Roman camp?'

'The one over there.'

'Oh, is there a Roman camp there?'

'Yes, the plaque says it dates from AD 65–160.'

He thought about this. 'So there was a Roman camp there in 1660?'

God, I thought, I can't let this guy look at my leg. 'Are you a doctor?'

'No, I'm an engineer, an electronics engineer.'

Says it all.

In despair, I turned to his unbadged companion, 'Will the bus take me back to Stanmore Tube station?' I asked the young man who had been listening to all of this.

'No, but it goes to Edgware.'

I had meant to go back to Stanmore to find All Saints' Church where Leefe Robinson, the first man to shoot down a zeppelin, is buried. Could I resist such an epitaph? My feet made the decision. The lure of Leefe and the rest of the Jubilee Line were to be pleasures foregone. I was going to Edgware, the Northern and my bed in Highgate.

CHAPTER FIVE

MORNINGTON PRESENCE

The bus from the Royal Orthopaedic Hospital dropped me at Edgware. Believing it to be a healthy beverage, I refreshed myself with a McDonald's milk shake (strawberry, if you must know) before limping through the columns of the station and on to the train.

At Burnt Oak station, which was marked 'For Watling', I noticed for the first time there were laurel bushes along the track. Maybe that is the only station to have them. I immediately thought of the old tradition of rewarding achievement with a laurel wreath. Maybe I was still in Roman mode.

Colindale is for the RAF museum, and I wanted to get off here but my feet wouldn't let me. Tomorrow would be soon enough.

As we drew in to Brent Cross station, I noticed a most peculiar triangle of houses almost totally hemmed in by roads. I wanted to go and look at that, too. But the distances from stations back to places that you've noticed on the line can be deceptive and I didn't think I could walk it. I kept remembering the long walk from Highgate station to the friend's house where I was staying. I had to keep some feet in reserve for that.

At last – or rather, all too soon – we were at Highgate and I *had* to walk again, into Archway Road. If I had walked back down the road towards Archway station, I might have seen the Archway, which was built to take Hornsey Lane over Archway Road, which is also the A1 Great North Road, allowing traffic to avoid the steep Highgate Hill. The first archway was built by Nash in 1813. This was replaced by the Binnie arch in 1900. But I walked the other way past a launderette that I hadn't noticed before. It sported the slogan Wishee-Washee, Splishee-Sploshee, Cleanee-Knickee, Vellee-Quickee. Very un-Highgate, I thought. Except for the Quickee. Many a shopkeeper would have Americanised that into Kwikee.

That thought sent me pleasantly to sleep that night.

The next day, I set out to visit the places my feet had boldly refused to go the day before and to explore the farther reaches of the Northern Line. I did so with some trepidation, not on account of my feet which had made a remarkable recovery but because the Northern Line is probably the most difficult one to explore logically because of the number of its branches. This arose from its amalgamation of two separate early underground railways and a section that used to be part of a mainline system.

Indeed, part of the Northern Line, opened in 1890 (ironically as the City and South London Railway) for three-and-a-quarter miles from King William Street to Stockwell, was the world's first underground electric railway. It was also London's first deep level tube. The fare was tuppence. As I keep reminding you, I had been buying day tickets for £3.80 and, as this was also to take me back to Heathrow that evening, I reckoned I was getting my travel cheaper than the Victorians.

The other original part of the Northern Line system was the bit that went northwards – the Charing Cross, Euston and Hampstead Railway, which opened in 1907. Under the auspices of the London Electric Railway in the 1920s, the lines were extended north to Edgware and south to Morden (which is still the most southerly point served by the Underground and the location of the largest train depot). It wasn't until 1937 that the whole system was renamed the Northern Line, by which time it had started to extend its other northern tentacle on the branch which I was currently exploring.

As Archway is convenient for Highgate Cemetery, I started there – the place where, in 1959, pop mega-star and millionaire, Rod Stewart, had worked as a gravedigger for £7.9s.4d per week. The western part of the graveyard is the more attractive but can only be visited by joining a guided tour. But Highgate is reckoned to be the most impressive cemetery this side of the Valley of the Kings, so it's well worth the effort. Among countless fascinating graves, you can then see those of Michael Faraday, and that latter-day scientist, Jacob Bronowski, as well as Nero the lion sitting on the tomb of circus performer, George Wombwell.

Of all the graveyard tales that emerge from Highgate, the most romantic, and most gruesome, concerns poet Dante Gabriel Rossetti, and his beautiful lover, Lizzie Siddall, whom Millais had immortalised on canvas as Ophelia. Like Shakespeare's tragic heroine, Lizzie, too, committed suicide. Distraught, Rossetti buried her with the love poems she had inspired in him plaited in her magnificent hair. Unfortunately, he had forgotten to take a copy. Seven years later, penniless, he decided to have her dug up again to retrieve his works for publication. This his friends did by the light of a bonfire. It is said that Lizzie looked as beautiful as ever. More extraordinary still, her hair had continued to grow so that it filled the entire coffin. Rossetti made £800 out of the poems. But the exhumation so haunted him that he insisted that he be buried anywhere but in Highgate.

As a postscript, the story is said to have so fascinated Bram Stoker that he based his famous exhumation scene from Dracula on it.

Given this wealth of interest, it is odd that most people choose to visit the eastern side where Karl Marx is interred.

From Highgate, I took the curious one-station branchlet to Mill Hill East, built in 1941, to find out why. Astonishingly, there was nothing there, not even a row of shops. I suppose you might point out there was a gasworks beside the track as we approached the station – but that didn't seem worthy of investigation.

I wondered if Mill Hill East was the location of a secret wartime government command centre bunker. The station is next to the gasworks, but to the north are (or were) Inglis Barracks and Mill Hill Barracks. I'll bet there's a bunker under that lot. Certainly the branch must have been important to someone, as they went to great efforts to build it. The railway viaduct at Dollis Brook, which carries the line over Dollis Road, is the highest point on the entire Underground system – 60 feet above ground level.

And that contrasts nicely with the opposite statistic – that the Northern Line also boasts the deepest point below ground level, at Holly Bush Hill, Hampstead. There, you would have to dig to a depth of 221 feet before stumbling across this remarkable tube. The station itself is 192 feet below ground level, and has the deepest lift shaft on the Underground at 181 feet.

We may as well get the statistics out of the way by also

mentioning that the Underground's deepest point below mean sea level, 70 feet, is also on the Northern Line – just south of Waterloo.

I travelled back to Finchley Central to pick up the High Barnet branch, which was extended there in 1940. Finchley Central has an interesting cast-iron bridge which leads out to a quiet street of shops and a Korean restaurant. No signs of war here, either.

High Barnet is one of those satisfying termini – the line stops dead here. At some of the other end-of-the-line stations, although the 'Underground' service comes to an end, the track itself carries on and is used by British Rail. At these places there is not the same satisfaction of achievement, of a journey completed. At High Barnet, there is. Beyond the buffers at the end of the line there is a thick copse of trees – I could distinguish sycamores and silver birches – and there was no doubt that this was the end of the system. High Barnet itself was as quiet as Mill Hill East. It was just a nice, peaceful, suburb.

Barnet Horse Fair, every September, gave rise to one of the more obscure pieces of Cockney rhyming slang – 'barnet' for 'hair'. Started in the Elizabethan times, it is still held to this very day.

Back at Camden Town, where in the mid-1920s the original two parts of the Northern Line joined together, I changed trains yet again – this time to retrace my steps back to Colindale. The RAF Museum is clearly signposted, but it is some walk from the Tube station. Thank goodness I didn't attempt it last night, I thought. Albatross Drive seemed to be a rather unfortunate choice of name to hang round anyone's neck, but it seemed that some of the newer housing estates had flying themes. They really should have been a bit more careful. Especially as the first thing that you see as you walk into the museum grounds is a boat! It is a 68-foot rescue and target towing launch manufactured by Vosper Thorneycroft. I wonder what the Royal Navy thought of that. But I suppose they had aircraft, so presumably it was quits. Evidently the RAF operated a large fleet of differing types of seacraft. Based at coastal stations (naturally), they were used to ferry men and supplies to and from flying boats. As the use of those wonderfully elegant technological pterodactyls declined, so did the RAF's sea fleet.

There are plenty of 'planes at Colindale as well, of course. There is the inevitable Spitfire – a Supermarine Mark VII – sitting outside as a 'gate guardian'. But, disappointingly, it is a copy in fibreglass. Under cover there are at least 70 'planes, from the earliest apparently constructed of string, paper and glue, to modern Phantoms and versatile Harriers. The whole impressive display belies the rather tatty buildings in which everything is housed.

The train on the way back to town contained the first signs that I had seen of urban guerrilla warfare against the Tube. Little printed stickers pasted over the internal ads proclaimed 'Spot fines are unenforceable, don't pay' and 'Fare dodging isn't a cheap thrill, it's an economic necessity'. The final message announced that 'London Underground treats its workers and passengers like shit'.

In the 1970s, the *Evening Standard*, as it was then called, ran a campaign about the dreadfully run-down state of the Northern Line. It's taken 20 years for something to be done about it. But the wait will be worth while. The previous rolling stock was mostly of 1959 vintage, red-painted trains manufactured by Metro–Cammell of Birmingham. In 1972, some new rolling stock, aluminium, light and airy, was introduced, but it was basically old technology. Now, they're building a major state-of-the-art signalling system and a fleet of similar trains, although the rate of investment is inevitably curtailed by financial considerations.

Golders Green is where most of the Northern Line trains are overhauled and maintained. But it was disappointingly non–Jewish. I saw one guy in a beard and Homburg walking up Golders Green Road. A few minutes later I saw another in a shop buying sweets. Or was it the same one? I would never make the mistake of claiming that they all look the same to me. But their drab, black uniform does make it difficult to tell them apart, which is, I suppose, the point. But those two were, disappointingly for someone in search of traditional, ethnic London, about all the Jewishness that I could detect.

What there is, is an amazingly cheap Chinese restaurant. Self-service, you can have the works – including spare ribs and barbecued crispy duck – for under £10, if you manage to fight your way through the scrum round the self-service table. And that includes the drink that they urge you to buy to 'allow them to keep the price of food down'. They also announce that they will not serve water as a first drink. Chinese tea at 80p is the cheapest way round this.

The restaurant was described as 'Hainanese'. Asking what kind of food that was, I was told that it was not a food style, but an island. Naturally, I thought that the owner must come from there. 'Oh no,' I was told, 'nobody comes from there. It's a terrible place, far too hot.' But if you check the Chinese wok-books you will see recipes for Hainanese dishes, so I don't think she knew what she was talking about.

There was a place much nearer than the South China Sea that I thought must be terrible. That was those flats I could see just north of Brent Cross. I went back.

From the station, I walked beside the dual carriage Hendon Way back along the tracks. A narrow walkway runs along the viaduct that takes the tracks over the North Circular Road. As you come off this walkway, you come to these ghastly houses. Ten yards from the viaduct, or 12 paces, because I paced it out. Outside of these rotting, peeling houses is the pretentious sign 'Clive Lodge Private Estate'. Private it may be, but a lodge it never was. It is a triangular block of decaying flats. Some are empty. Some hide sticks of furniture behind dirty curtains and broken venetian blinds. There is a stream running alongside which you would expect to be filthy. But the water is completely clear. The roads are in good condition. And the traffic on the motorway runs freely. Private squalor, public wealth. What would Prince Charles say?

On the way back, a jogger in a Glasgow University tee-shirt ran past me. But I was too depressed by the housing to check if he were genuine.

As an antidote, I set out to have a look at Hampstead Heath. From the station, a beautiful, old-fashioned affair with gleaming dark green tiles around the ticket windows, I walked up Heath Street, which is just a village high street, along Spaniards Road and on to the heath. It was just what had been promised – a huge chunk of countryside with a great view right across London to Canary Wharf. Walking northwards up Spaniards Road, I drank in the size of the houses – and the palm trees that decorated the gardens. I came across Jack Straw's Castle, a two-storey, wooden inn named after one of Wat Tyler's hench-persons. Just before the road plunges down Hampstead Lane is another romantically named pub, Spaniard's Inn. Further down the Lane is Kenwood House. Sitting in massive grounds, this is a bequest to the nation by Lord Iveagh, complete with extensive picture galleries.

Walking back down steep Heath Street, I realised that it was the variety of the houses that gave Hampstead its village look. The Quakers' Meeting House in black-and-white, with a half dome above the entrance, could have come off a film set.

The Hotel La Gaffe, with its wooden-framed windows and its little house on the wall for the menu, its wicker chairs and its coffee machines, was the most authentic Italian café I have seen for some time. Across the road, Giuliano's was modern, square, cream. But its window boxes and its palm tree in a pot made it authentic, too, in its own way. And it was sheer delight to gaze up Hollybush steps at Holly Mount House. Very villagey.

I called it a day.

Perhaps the greatest disappointment of my Tube travels was not being able to stand in Mornington Crescent. That station had been shut for a £7 million refurbishment many months before my trek, and wasn't due to be opened for years. All I got was the tantalising view of the station signs as the train slowed down to negotiate the sepulchral gloom.

This was one station that I wanted to visit, not for its architecture, not for its position on the network, not for what London treasures lay above, but for its own sake. Because Mornington Crescent had given its name to a radio game that rivals *The Archers* in its popularity. And I had followed it since its inception as part of Radio Four's *I'm Sorry, I Haven't a Clue* in 1973.

The attraction of the game lies in the obscurity, arbitrariness and randomness of the rules. It is the lbw law of radio quizzes. The only person who is prepared to parade a pretence of understanding them is a founder member of the panel, Graeme Garden. For beginners, he explains them thus: 'The game's origins were in a comics' club in the West End in the Sixties, when a bloke came in and said he had just been taught this wonderful game. He said that people sat around and named Tube stations and the first person to say "Mornington Crescent" won.

'For a perfect win, a player has to say "Mornington Crescent" just before the next person was going to say it. Now, even the abridged version of the rules, sub-rules and codicils would fill many volumes if anyone could publish them. The rules have been collated by several authorities. Unfortunately, to be an authority you have to publish your rules immediately before the next person was going to publish them, so there are a lot of unpublished authorities.' That's English humour.

For an altogether different, now traditional game, The Angel, Islington, is one of the cheapest properties on the Monopoly board. In real life, its Tube station is modern and deep. £70 million has been spent on building a new, larger station with two platforms instead of the former single 'island'. Angel has the longest escalator on the Underground system, and, indeed, in Europe: 66 yards long, it takes 80 seconds to transport a passenger up and down the 30–foot drop. The marble walls went on and on as I ascended to the street. Outside, like so many of the stations nowadays, the space above housed a new office and shopping complex.

I didn't expect to be amused at Angel. But it should have been called after a miracle, or a monument, at least. To find that the station takes its name from a pub is a disappointment. It is doubly so to discover that the pub is long gone and that the Corner House which replaced it in 1921 was itself replaced by a bank.

At least The Angel had a bit of history. It was famous enough as a stop-over for coach travellers for Dickens to mention it in *Oliver Twist*. When Noah Claypole and Charlotte arrive at the inn they 'wisely judged from the crowd of passengers and number of vehicles that London began in earnest'.

Some claim that Thomas Paine, the radical, wrote *The Rights of Man*, which was published in 1782, in The Angel Inn. Others say it was the Old Red Lion. Maybe he was on a pub crawl at the time.

A short walk down City Road from Old Street station is Bunhill Fields cemetery, burial ground for more than 5,000 victims of the Great Plague of 1665. The trees grow stronger and greener here. William Blake and Daniel Defoe are also buried here. As is John Lettsom, the Quaker who introduced the mangel-wurzel to England.

Coming out of a chaotic London Bridge station, totally disrupted by the construction of the extension of the Jubilee Line, I eventually stumbled on to Duke Street and, looking for the river, found myself outside Southwark Cathedral. One of the guidebooks I had been scanning in a Glasgow bookshop as part of my pre-journey research (!) told me that Southwark used to be beyond the city limits, 'the place to which criminals, actors and other undesirables were banished'.

From what I could glean from the same source, the church itself is the oldest Gothic building in London. It is noted for its choir and retro-choir. The transepts are fifteenth century, but the huge nave was redesigned in Victorian times and echoes the original. And it was upgraded from a parish church to a cathedral only in 1905. But I was not there for the architecture – nor even for the religion – but for the food! Or rather, for the restaurant. I had been told that the refurbished Chapter House contained a fast food outlet. I didn't believe it and wanted to check it out for myself.

I turned the corner of the cathedral and there was the sign, Pizza Express. So it was true. There was nothing for it but to go in and have a pizza. The menu was the standard one for that firm, but it was presented on a tasteful, mediaeval manuscript-type form. The food and the service were excellent.

On the way out I collected a brochure entitled *Eat at Cathedrals and Churches*, which proclaimed itself to be 'a guide to ecclesiastical restaurants around Britain'. You could eat in the coffee shop after Benediction in Bath, or sample scouse with red cabbage at Matins on Merseyside. In all there are 36 churches up and down the country offering corporal as well as spiritual refuelling. Most are shut on Good Friday. Presumably there is not much trade on a day when traditionally Christians have been exhorted to fast and abstain.

The directory had been produced by the Association of Ecclesiastical Caterers which, the blurb told me, was formed 'in order that Refectory Managers could share experience and information in this, their particular and unique area of commercial catering'. Their mission statement (surely the most apt use of this American management jargon?) claimed that members are linked by 'our common interest in the ministry of welcome'. 'We are not an official trade association,' the message went on, 'and are not bound by a code of practice.' But by something much more enduring – though, for consumers in the short run, much less enforceable.

Replete, I left the restaurant irreverently wondering if there was a holy water font in the toilets. I wanted to walk the river bank to see

97

the restoration work that had been in progress for some years. In front of me was a demasted old schooner, the *Kathleen and May*, in dry dock. Its deck was tarpaulined over and it was totally deserted. Was this the sister ship of the *Mary Celeste*? It might well have been, but exhaustive efforts to find out more, from every organisation that I could think might be responsible for it, from the Port of London Authority to the London Tourist Board, drew a blank.

I was on my way to jail.

The original clink is here in Clink Street. Now restored and a museum, this was the prison whose name entered the language.

I wandered on beside the broad river to the Anchor Inn, which looked old and historic. Inside, it captured the atmosphere that most tourists identify with an English pub, but I couldn't find out much about its history. It housed the *Financial Times* bar. But that was locked and empty.

As I left, I passed an attractive blonde in her late thirties, I guessed, coming in. I was only ten yards away when she called to me: 'I wonder if you could take our picture.' As I obliged, she told me that the man she was posing with had been at school with her 30 years ago and that this was their first meeting since then. It had been a series of coincidences that had put them in touch with each other again and they had decided to meet. 'Life's like that,' she observed. He, thinning on top and generally not wearing as well as her, rather sadly agreed.

Further up river is the Globe Theatre, or Shakespeare's Globe, to give it its marketing title. This completely newly built Elizabethan theatre was the brainchild of the late Sam Wanamaker, the American film director. I found it of no interest to discover how sixteenth-century craftsmen went about their work and so simply circled the outside. While it is of academic interest to see how plays had to work in that kind of setting, I am not convinced that re-running them there today will add anything to the enjoyment. Theatrical production has moved a long way since then, and for the better. Just a little bit up river is a much better prospect for an arts centre. It's a huge derelict brick power station. They'd have been better putting the money into that. At least they can't convert it to more yuppie flats. It's got no windows.

The original Globe, built in Southwark in 1599, was where

Shakespeare's masterpieces were first performed. It had a much shorter life than his immortal lines, being destroyed by fire after an accident with a stage cannon during a performance of *Henry VIII*. The first failed attempt at virtual reality entertainment. The effect was later perfected by Tchaikovsky for his 1812 overture.

That's enough Shakespeare, so 'Let us make an honourable retreat; though not with bag and baggage, yet with scrip and scrippage'. Or, more succinctly, 'Sweets to the sweet: farewell!' as Hamlet put it to Ophelia.

I got back on to the Northern Line at London Bridge and headed south. This part of the Tube, all the way to Colliers Wood, follows a line directly under the A24 trunk road . . . Borough High Street to Elephant & Castle, now little more than a major traffic roundabout . . . Kennington Park Road to The Oval, London's other Test cricket ground . . . Clapham Road towards the Common, . . . under Balham High Road and Tooting High Street . . . 16 miles, more or less straight, completely traffic–free under the streets.

Part of this section was opened in 1890 as an isolated stretch of Tube, from King William Street north of the river, not far from Pudding Lane, to Stockwell. King William Street was closed in 1900 when a new tunnel under the Thames, via London Bridge, linked the southern section from Borough to the northern section at Moorgate. I wonder what the original tunnel is used for these days, if at all.

The mythical Man on the Clapham Omnibus, in my view, should have taken to the Tube long ago, such is the appalling traffic snarl-up of that area which must, surely, delay all surface transport journeys.

I'd never visited Balham before, but I could not avoid doing so to check on the only conscious image of the place I have in my mind. That was created for me by the late Peter Sellers, with one of his earliest nonsense records. *Balham, Gateway to the South* must have entered the hit parade in the Fifties. It certainly caught on with my pals, with its curious mixture of echoes of Rupert Brooke and John Betjeman.

Four square upon the Northern Line
Stands Balham, Gateway to the South . . .
The Town Hall clock says ten-to-three.
But is there honey still for tea?

Is there a tea-shop in Balham any more? I didn't see one.

One of the oddest names on the Underground must be Tooting Bec. Even odder is that this is the location of the second largest outdoor swimming pool in Europe. It's exactly 100 yards long. Where is the largest? Not on the Underground. Tooting Bec Lido is at the end of Tooting Bec Lido Road, of course, beside Tooting Bec Common. But it's only open from late-May to September.

Open all the year round at Tooting Broadway is St George's Hospital, which is one of London's great teaching hospitals. You emerge from the Underground station on the corner of Tooting High Street and Mitcham Road, two undistinguished and indistinguishable south London 'thoroughfares', certainly not broad ways, but typical of so many others, with anonymous shops on either side, separated from the busy single highway by inadequate pavements. No character here whatsoever. And, six side streets away to the south-west, tucked behind more of the ubiquitous London brick terraces, is this enormous, sprawling, 1970s concrete-and-glass edifice, St George's Hospital, relocated lock, stock and CT scanner from its original site and magnificent building at Hyde Park Corner.

South again, unaware of what attractions, if any, the rural-sounding Colliers Wood had to offer above ground. And on again. I knew that Wimbledon was a fairly classy area. But if that were so, then it declines dramatically as you turn into Merton Road. I would have thought that South Wimbledon would have been even more upmarket, but it was really rather grotty. The Tube station was one of the familiar art-deco type with the classic Underground sign that so many stations have managed to retain. There were two notices inside. One promised big expenditure over the next seven years on upgrading the Northern Line. The other, which talked about making the system safer by the installation of video cameras, for the first time made me feel nervous on the Tube, by raising worries that I had never had.

The Tube is a fairly crime-free environment. Since the introduction in 1987 of a variety of security measures, crime statistics have fallen by 40 per cent. The measures taken on the Northern Line were the most effective. They needed to be: the southern end of the Northern had the highest violent crime rate per passenger of any on the system. They introduced 'control or focal points', large glass-fronted offices where highly-visible staff monitored what was going on through closed-circuit television. Green emergency buttons along the station connect directly to the Underground branch of the British Transport Police – a kind of secret service, I guess. As ever, improvements are made as money allows.

Morden station is one of the first they should spend money on. Right away, it could do with a good wash. The façade might once have been impressive, but the glass and blue plastic offices which have been built around it give it a cheap tacky look. This turned out to be symptomatic of Morden's history. Here there was no prehistoric settlement, and neither the Romans nor the Saxons rated it. With the result that, by 1086, the Doomsday Book recorded its size as only eight villains, five cottars and a serf. You can imagine the life *he* had.

CHAPTER SIX

SIGNS AND SIGNALS

Richmond is the usual rich, busy, traffic-ridden town. If you've arrived by Underground, of course, you wouldn't know where it was, other than it's in the bottom left-hand corner of the Underground map. In fact, you don't *need* to know where you are – and this is one of the charms of travelling by Underground, it has its own virtual reality. Its map is all you need, unrelated to real geography. There were a number of occasions on my journeys when I was actually disappointed to catch sight of a road sign, which brought me back to the spatial reality of the rest of Britain. The Underground, however, cocoons you in its own universe, its own time–space continuum.

But, I was told, Richmond is on the Surrey fringes of metropolitan London.

The building which caught my attention was an old fire station from 1870, with a clock and a bell tower above the clock. The modern extension behind it blends correctly, and a pleasing sensation of a conversion well done is concluded by the tasteful tenancy of the ground floor by one of those shops that look good but in which you can't actually find anything that you would want to buy. Grand Illusions is an upmarket Habitat offering dozens of things that you can't see anybody buying . . . . like soap in the shape and colour of a gull's egg, or a plain-painted empty cardboard box, or a vertical mallard drake. The illusion is spoiled by the shop next door. Under a crude black-and-white shop sign, it sells garish clothes for women. Somehow, I didn't have a picture of scarlet ladies inhabiting this part of Surrey.

Richmond may once have been a market town, but the current market is tiny. The biggest stall is for fish. The smell permeates the rest of the place, including the café. The rest of the market consists of two flower stalls, two fruiterers and a few shops selling tee-shirts and greetings cards.

I felt peckish, and spotted a pizza parlour. Pizzas are my favourite fast food, the ethnic food which I think travels best across the world. So I decided to market test Richmond's Pizzaland for comparison with the holy dish I had partaken of in Southwark Cathedral. But the service was so good that it reminded me of the quiz show which you have to participate in before you get your breakfast in America. Freshly jet-lagged the morning after getting off the transatlantic 'plane, you sit yourself down, desperate for a decent bit of food. But it's like *Twenty Questions*, a multiple choice version, with the answers recorded on a big pad.

'Hi! How are you today?'

'Fine, thank you.'

'That's good. What juice would you like today? We have orange, apple, tomato, grapefruit, grape or prune.'

'Orange, please.'

'OK. Is that large, medium or regular?'

'Large, please.'

'OK. Would you like toast?'

'Yes, please.'

'OK. Do you want white, wholemeal or rye?'

'Wholemeal, please.'

'OK. Dark or light?'

'Dark, please.'

'OK. Would you like eggs?'

'Yes, please.'

'OK. Is that one or two?'

'Two, please.'

'OK. Brown or white?'

'Does it matter?'

'I'm sorry?'

'White, please.'

'OK. Regular or low-cholesterol?'

'What's a low-cholesterol egg? Never mind. Regular.'

'OK. Boiled, fried or scrambled?'

'Fried.'

'OK. Do you want them easy over or sunny side up?'

103

'. . . STOP,' I long to cry,'just bring me my breakfast. And while you're doing it, don't comment on my "cute" accent or ask me where I'm from.'

Yes, I know it's my bad temper again. It comes from having low blood sugar levels because these maddeningly polite people won't feed me. And while I am on about food how *can* a civilised people add bacon to blueberry pancakes and then pour maple syrup over both?

Paradise Road is a disappointment. It doesn't live up to its name. But a plaque tells me that Leonard and Virginia Woolf lived there. Did you know that there was a Leonard? And was anyone ever afraid of him?

I wandered around searching for the poppy factory that was marked on the map. Onslow Avenue Mansions form a long impressive terrace – rather like an old English seaside hotel, all pillars and balconies. Built in 1905, they are no longer large town houses but small flats. Opposite them, what had been a series of joined-up red-brick semis were effectively disguised by white and cream paint. Otherwise they would have looked like North of England red-brick terraces. But I suppose you need the sunshine to carry off the light colours.

Rounding a corner coming into Richmond Hill, I was confronted by a four-storey castle with turrets and arrow slits. Only a ball occasionally bouncing above an exaggeratedly high wall announces that it is, in fact, a school. There is no notice to that effect, even at the front entrance. I was pleased to see that, even this far south and this far up the social ladder, the kids were playing football at playtime. But I was to be disappointed. The reason the ball kept rising into view was that it was aimed not at a goal but at a hoop, and they were playing basketball. No wonder we struggle to qualify for the World Cup.

Eventually, I found the poppy factory. The main entrance was closed. Open at two o'clock, the notice said. I had 15 minutes to kill, so I wandered around. The monotonous clanking of machines indicated that something was being manufactured, but the windows were too high to see what. I came back to the main entrance and saw that a group of pensioners were sitting in the foyer, listening to a lecture. I sat outside in the sun waiting for the office to open, somewhat apprehensively. A long tour looked in prospect.

I hate tours of such places and long-winded explanations about fairly mundane mechanical functions. I was looking for a quick chat, a PR hand-out and off. Two o'clock and the office staff trailed back into work. A friendly secretary asked if she could help and took me in through the canteen. I was introduced to Ray Webb who would supply my needs. Ray had been a training corporal in the now disbanded East Surrey Regiment. He had served in Cyprus during the EOKA troubles. Now aged 59, he was a stock control liaison manager at the factory. And guide.

I told him very slowly and clearly that I had a meeting back in London shortly and that I just needed some basic information, an overview.

He took me into the showroom and began: 'Over there you see Colonel John McCrae, who was a Canadian soldier. He wrote a poem when he was in the trenches during the Second Battle of Eye–eper which started on 22 April 1915. He wrote the poem on 3 May 1915. The poem was called *Flanders Fields* and it talked about the poppies which grew there. It asked the people back home to be faithful to the sacrifices that the soldiers were making.'

I have never been to Guelph, Ontario, where McCrae was born. But I have been to Fergus which is as hick as its name suggests. It was an official visit, and the British Tourist Authority underestimated the time it would take to get from Bloor Street, in downtown Toronto, to Fergus. We were an hour and a half late, and when we arrived the kilted reception committee were lying about drunk on the grass outside the Scottish Society's headquarters. They enjoyed my visit thoroughly.

'An American lady, Moina Michael – that's her over there – read the poem and she began wearing a poppy as an act of faith. She worked at Columbia University. One day she was holding a party in her house – she did voluntary work for the YMCA – for some friends who had come over to America. As usual, she was wearing a poppy. Someone asked her what it was for. She told them about Colonel John McCrae and the poem. And one of her guests at the party gave her a small donation. She said that she would go into New York to buy them all a poppy. She did that and came back with 25 poppies which she gave out.'

I looked round the showroom. A sign indicated that the number of visitors to date that year had been 1,689. I would be visitor number 1,690. My West of Scotland acquaintances would have a wry chuckle.

Ray was into it now. 'One of the guests was a French lady called Madame Guerin. She went back to France and started the idea of raising money for disabled ex-servicemen by selling artificial poppies. That's Madame Guerin.'

I tried to end the interview by thanking Ray, but he was in full flow.

'The British Legion was formed after World War I. The four service associations were merged to make it. It held the first Poppy Day in 1921. On the 11th of November to be exact, exactly three years after the ceasefire. Over £100,000 was raised.

'But these poppies were made in France and they wanted to find somewhere in England to make them. Major George Howson MC had been in the war and he wanted to help disabled ex–servicemen. So he approached Earl Haig and asked if he could make the poppies.'

My mind wandered from the rehearsed phrases. How could Haig – who had condemned so many millions to horror, deprivation and death – be tolerated, never mind respected, by those who had managed to survive the worst that he could do to them? I thought about the scene in *Oh What a Lovely War*. 'Why do you keep sending these men over the top?' Haig is asked. 'Because our rate of attrition is half of the Germans. If it goes on like this, they shall have 5,000 men left and we shall have 10,000. And we shall win.' Win we did, and he got an earldom instead of being thrown in jail as a criminal.

Ray's voice intruded on my thoughts: 'Major Howson was given £2,000 by the British Legion to make the poppies. He established a factory in the Old Kent Road. But he wasn't sure that it was going to be successful. He wrote to his parents, "I do not think it can be a great success, but it is worth trying." He moved the factory down here after 1925 when he was employing over 150 men and needed more space.'

'Excuse me, Ray,' I interrupted again. 'What are those big wooden crosses?'

'Oh, those are original crosses, taken from the Somme.'

The casual remark, delivered in the same voice as the rest of the lecture, stopped me short. This wasn't a factory tour. This wasn't a job creation scheme for the physically–challenged. This was a memorial to millions of fathers and sons who did their duty and never came back. I remembered that my father's brother had died in France. Having survived years in the trenches, he had his legs amputated by the train he fell under on his way back from the front. He died the next day. 'Mama never recovered,' my father said.

'Ray,' I said, 'If you've got time, I'd like to see round.'

The factory, converted from a brewery, is old-fashioned but is as efficiently laid out as is possible on three floors. There are very noisy areas where plastic is extruded to make the green stems of the poppies. There are less noisy areas where machines clank out the red petals and the green oak leaves and where the small wooden crosses of remembrance are cut out and pieced together. There are quiet areas where the custom-made wreaths which are laid by members of the Royal Family are assembled. And, of course, every town and city in the United Kingdom is supplied with its wreaths for its own local ceremony.

The factory produces 34 million poppies every year. It produces 2.4 million petals which rain down on the audience at the Albert Hall during the annual Festival of Remembrance. Apart from the poppies themselves, the factory makes special products . . . . poppy sprays, crosses, wreaths and so on. Not many people know, for example, that a wreath is taken abroad on most foreign Royal visits.

Ray saw me to the door and beyond. 'I'm interested in doing research on Madame Guerin,' he told me. 'I have written to the French government and the French Embassy, but they didn't bother to reply. So I took a day off and went up to the library at the Embassy. But there was nothing there. I was told she's just not a historical figure in France.'

There's not much more you want to do in Richmond after that experience. So I didn't seek out Mrs Beeton's restaurant – nothing to do with her, but run by a co-operative of women who take turns at doing the cooking – or anything else which might have caught my eye. But I thought that I should at least look at the Thames.

The view from Richmond Bridge was the classic one – wide river, willow trees and wildlife. The archetypal picture was completed by the craftsman at Richmond Bridge Boathouses plying his traditional skills in boat-building. But the fact that he was talking on a mobile phone at the same time was possibly an indication that nowhere can you escape the pressure of modern business.

I was curious enough to go down from the bridge to find out what kind of boat he was working on. It was a Thames skiff, I was told, a traditional rowing boat for three rowers. It was only when I looked into the skiff that I realised that this was a special day, for there nestling in the bows was a bottle of champagne. The *Dick Offer* – named after the 'longest standing member', according to the club's captain – was about to be launched.

The boat's new varnish gleamed, and the craftsmanship made it look really expensive. I asked the man carrying the oars down to the river how much it cost. Nine thousand pounds, I was told. But you normally ordered three so that you would get matching boats which you could race. The person I was speaking to was Keith Shaw of The Skiff Club, which was celebrating its centenary year.

Jill had brought the champagne, but when she saw that the boatbuilder had supplied a bottle of inferior stuff, she sensibly decided to use that for the launch and save the better stuff to drink.

The launch was a fairly low-key affair. The boat on a two-wheeled bogey was pushed down the concrete slipway into the water. Jill, as instructed, poured the champagne over the bows (and over the hands of the boat-builder who was doing the pushing!). As the bogey slipped under the water at the end of a long rope, I wondered how you got it back. Wade in and get your feet wet? Wait for the tide to go out? But all trades have their tricks. With a satisfyingly deft flick of his wrist this master craftsman freed the skiff to float off and drew the bogey back up the ramp.

I then asked Jill about the history of the club, telling her that I was writing about the area. 'You'd better speak to Graeme, he's the president.' But I didn't want to intrude further on what was a special day for them, and walked away. I hadn't got back to the road when Graeme caught up with me. 'Jill tells me that you are writing an article. What do you want to know?' Ah, the power of the press.

In late Victorian times there were about 3,000 skiffs available for hire on the Thames (the famous *Three Men in a Boat* rented one) and regattas were common. The boats were derivatives of commercial craft adapted for pleasure and for racing. Now there are four major and two minor clubs on the Thames. There are double skiffs of the kind I saw being launched with two people pulling and a cox. And singles with one rower and no cox. They race two kinds of race . . . short ones over 600 metres (not yards, even although skiff racing is a purely English sport) and marathons over three to four miles (or, presumably, five kilometres). The club has 100, mainly social, members and 12 boats, the oldest of which was built in 1927.

I walked quickly back through the town anxious to be on to my next stop. The only thing I noted was the Union Jack tee-shirt in the window with the legend 'England'. Not for the first time, I asked silently why the English can't be more careful about such matters. It was Robert Burns who first noted this irritating tendency for the English to use 'England' when they mean England *and* when they mean Britain. 'Nothing,' he wrote, 'can reconcile me to the common terms English Ambassador, English Court, etc.'

It was the Scots that took the Union seriously, with genteel Edinburgh ladies addressing their letters as from 'North Britain'. The English never adopted the equivalent 'South Britain' because, of course, to them it wasn't a union it was a take-over. Not that they did that in a malicious way. It just seemed obvious. And it still does today, which is one reason why we have trouble with Scottish nationalism.

I mulled this over as I sat waiting for the train to leave, staring out at the wrought-iron stanchions that support the station roof. As the train left, I had another bizarre thought. Just outside Richmond station are some beautiful new houses built of light-coloured brick, with balconies – that face the tracks! For train spotters only, surely!

Kew Gardens station has not only got similar roof supports to those at Richmond, but also a wrought-iron extension which houses a comfortable pub. The station building itself is two storeys of white London brick with rough-cast chimneys . . . a little house that would look more at home in a children's novel or in more rural surroundings – which could have been how it started out.

I had spotted an absurd, but effective, advertisement for Kew Gardens on the Tube. 'Stroll around Kew Gardens 3 billion years before it opens.' So, expecting dinosaurs to be treading the vegetation, I ventured across the road and through the elegant gates.

109

The first thing I noticed about the Royal Botanic Gardens, Kew, was the proliferation of daisies on the lawns. If they can't get rid of them, I thought, who can? The second thing, I was delighted to see, was that there were no 'Keep off the Grass' signs anywhere.

One in eight of all flowering species – including the daisies, presumably – are grown at Kew. George III might have been mad, but he helped establish the most famous gardens since Nebuchadnezzar landscaped Babylon. There is no way of covering all of the gardens' 300 acres in one visit, so you just have to pick your favourite flora and make a start.

The King, who later had to carry the can for losing the American colonies, made an investment here which has repaid Britain handsomely, and in unforeseen ways. The story is told of one enterprising Englishman, Sir Henry Wickham, who saw the colossal fortunes that the Portuguese were making out of the rubber plantations in Brazil. Not only were the planters able to build an opera house in the middle of the rain forests, but, maybe an even better indicator of their wealth, every month they sent their laundry all the way home from Manaus to Portugal. On the instructions of the British government, Wickham loyally risked smuggling rubber tree seeds out of Brazil. Some were taken to Kew and some to the Physic Garden in Chelsea. They germinated and were grown on under glass at Kew. But, of course, needing a hot, moist environment they could not be grown commercially in Britain. So they were transported to the Empire's possessions in South East Asia, and, in the late nineteenth century Malaya became the centre of the world's production of natural rubber.

The rose garden was the place for me to see how the English handled their national emblem – which is more than the Scots can do. On the way there, I passed one of the many heraldic statues. The one that particularly caught my eye was the Greyhound of Richmond, which looked like a model of the children's cartoon character, Scooby Doo. The rose garden itself was a disappointment, with little in bloom. In fact this was true of the whole place. There was a distinct lack of riotous, colourful, blooming display. Perhaps June is between seasons. Perhaps the Palm House – 'a unique masterpiece of Victorian engineering' – would be more exciting. I pushed through the heavy door and carefully shut it as instructed. It was certainly quiet. I had the place to myself. It was steamy. It was hot. It was everything a rain forest should be. There were not only palms, but other tropical plants, including rubber plants, from all over the world. The only nagging distraction was a distant bell coming, it seemed, from beneath my feet.

As I wandered to the door to leave, it burst open and in dashed three firemen with that happy look of eagerness that comes from boredom interrupted. 'And what are you doing here, *sir*?' It was too complicated to try to explain that no one had stopped me going in and that the bell didn't really sound like a fire alarm. So I contented myself with remarking that, if you were going to be caught in a fire, a tropical rain forest was probably as safe a place as any.

Outside the Palm House is a beautiful long vista in the direction of Queen Charlotte's Cottage. It would make a beautiful golf course hole. You'd just have to cut down a couple of trees. An irreverent thought. And then I remembered the savaging which the trees in Kew Gardens had received in the famous storm of October 1987.

'There will be no hurricane tonight,' said the weatherman smugly on the television forecast. How wrong he was. During the night gales lashed the South of England damaging property and destroying woodlands. London's parks were devasted as centuries-old trees were blown down throughout the Home Counties, Kew alone lost ten per cent of its 9,000 trees but its sister garden in West Sussex had 20,000 irreparably damaged. Sadly, too, Sevenoaks in Kent had six of its seven trees blown down. These seven Turkey oaks had been planted in 1902 to mark the coronation of Edward VII. With commendable foresight the local council had, in 1945, agreed to a back-up team of a further seven trees being planted right across the road. These were a gift from Canadian airmen who had been stationed nearby during the war. Three of these were lost as well. There were mercifully only four deaths as wind swept through the affected area. If the storm had struck during the day the toll in human lives would have been much higher.

I walked the 50 yards or so to the Water-Lily House, which was being guarded by a policeman. A group hung about waiting to get in. One American tourist, either mistaking the policeman for a security guard or much more sure of his rights than the rest of us, approached the policeman and asked to be let in. 'Sorry, sir, there's a fire alert.'

'But, that's in the building over there.' 'Part of the same place, sir.' 'Don't be daft,' countered the bold foreigner. But he still didn't get in.

However, we only had to wait a few more minutes for the all-clear. Inside were exotic species of the useful variety – rudely-shaped gourds of shapes, loofahs and papyrus. Around the papyrus plant was strung, like decorations on a Christmas tree, pieces of Kleenex roll without the perforations. It wasn't clear whether the paper actually grew on the plant like that or was a graphic sample of the finished product.

It's an easy place to lose your sense of direction, despite the little map which comes with the entry price. I detoured on my way to the pagoda to have a look at King William's Temple, only to discover that it was the Temple of Bellona. The ground just to the right of it rose slightly uphill to what would make an interesting par three.

Though a non-drinker myself, I passed quickly through the Temperate House to the Evolution House which had been so well advertised on the Tube. There, the description of how life evolved from plants over a period of three-and-a-half billion years moves away from the factual into the realms of recreation, which is something better left to Disney. Now that we are blasé about the special effects of films such as *Jurassic Park*, it is difficult for such a static display as the one at Kew to be credible. The plastic dragonfly the size and stiffness of a model aeroplane is the worst example. But at least you could experience one Hollywood-type phenomenon at Kew. Remember those Tarzan movies with the hidden caves behind waterfalls? Well, at Kew, you can stand behind the waterfall in the Evolution House and peer through the water at the other visitors.

The Pagoda is a real disappointment. It doesn't even lean. And it has an even number of storeys, something that no self-respecting Chinese architect would contemplate. Missing are its original 80 iron dragons, sold by George IV to pay off his creditors. And it is this loss which may have detracted irreparably from the Pagoda's magic. Each lion was covered in glass and held a bell in its jaws, to provide the sound effects to a dazzling spectacle. None of this effect is conserved and so the whole thing is a bit of a let-down. The Pagoda was built as a birthday surprise by Sir William Chambers for the

Dowager Princess of Wales in 1762. The surprise now is that it isn't open, so you can't walk up it. All you can do is walk round it a couple of times, and then trudge the mile back to the main gate.

This took me past the flagpole – the tallest in the UK. Kew is twice as old as British Columbia, the sign said. I suppose most things in Britain are. The British Columbians displayed that affection for the mother country which is the hallmark of so many colonialists. When they came to provincehood, they incorporated the Union flag in their own. But they put the rayed sun above the Union Jack, when protocol dictated that nothing should have precedence over the British symbol. Red-faced, the loyal Canadians reversed their position on advice from London. But not before the stained-glass window in the provincial parliament building had been installed with the original design. Today, every tour guide in Victoria tells the story.

The flagpole came from a Douglas fir that originally weighed 37 tons, reduced to 15 tons at Kew, where it was shaped. It was erected in 1959 to celebrate the centennial of the Canadian province and the bi-centenary of Kew – even although they occurred in different years. What chance now of cutting down an old Douglas fir? With all the green protesters, we'll soon have difficulties cutting down Christmas trees.

Station Parade, Kew, is a row of varied and busy shops, including, naturally, many selling plants. I would have liked a New Guinea Busy Lizzy or a tobacco plant. But plants are just too awkward to carry. But I did take on board an excellent afternoon tea at the Kew Greenhouse – a little restaurant on the way back to the station.

Sliding into Gunnersbury, I noticed a brand new multi-storey car park, all designer entrances. I had seen a stylish one at Amersham, too, though it was of an entirely different design. The Underground has always placed great emphasis on the architecture of its stations. Is this now spilling over into the car parks which have naturally become a more and more important feature of suburban termini?

Getting off at Turnham Green and crossing to the other pair of platforms, I set off for the end of the District Line at Ealing Broadway. The train seemed brand new, with a different configuration of seats – two in and two out, which were narrower but more comfortable. The District Line was the first to introduce aluminium bodywork, in 1952. Its origins date back to 1868, but this particular branch was opened just 11 years later, two years after the extension to Richmond. And, in 1883 for a couple of years, the District Line trains were allowed to run over the Great Western Railway tracks to Windsor – presumably by Royal command!

With the exception of Chiswick Park (which boasts a quite delightful 'classical'-style station, inevitably preserved by an official listing), the branch line now runs to stations which are also on the northbound Piccadilly Line branch – until it gets to Ealing, when it veers off westwards to meet up with the Central Line terminus.

What I wanted to see at Ealing Broadway were the studios where British comedy first got an international bad name – though the British (or should that be English?) continue to exhibit a strange affection for all those dreadful films, including the *Carry On* series and all those *Doctor* films with trainee medics that all look over 40. I had been told that members of the public can arrange tours of Ealing studios, and they have regular open days, but this turned out not to be one of them.

All along the white wall of the studio was painted, in green and white script lettering, 'The Studio with Team Spirit'. On the road down to the studios is yet another university – this time, the University of Thames Valley.

Further into the town, the legend 'Walpole Picture Theatre' is emblazoned on a gable end. But I couldn't find the picture house itself. So I walked back to the station past a row of phone boxes at the corner of High Street and Ealing Green. There, propped up open in the middle box, was a pornographic magazine. Maybe this was the Walpole Picture Theatre?

I suspected a trap. Was this some kind of *Candid Camera* set-up, to see what different passers-by would do with the magazine. Best to walk on and ignore it. A few hundred yards later, I re-thought the position. Much better to pick it up and see what happened. Whatever it was, I could always write about it. And I could avoid any public embarrassment about looking at that kind of literature by proving that I was writing a book. So I went back for it and stuck it in my bag.

Nothing happened. I still don't know, of course, whether I was being secretly filmed or not. Maybe I'll suddenly pop up on *Beadle's*

About, clutching my – or rather, his – copy of *Penthouse*. Or maybe it was part of a research project by the University of Thames Valley. It's the kind of thing that new universities do, especially if they have Departments of Sociology.

Anyway, the photography was of a very high quality.

So is the Ealing Broadway Shopping Centre. It's one of the best I have been in. It's a comfortable size, built (or at least faced) in red brick, not concrete, and the design is warm and friendly with twin towers and a slightly nautical look. I particularly enjoyed the fact that it is part indoors and part outdoors, with a little park with wooden benches where you can relax and read your newspapers – or magazines. There are hanging baskets, rowan trees and sculptures of mothers, fathers and children – and a pleasant fountain and pool.

I know that banks are cathedrals to money. But Ealing has a bank converted from an English parish church – a wry comment on the shift from God to Mammon. But a sound investment for people like Robert Bevan of Barclay's Bank who, you will remember, built the church at Cockfosters. Here he was getting his investment back.

I boarded a train bound for Upminster, the far end of the District Line, but I had other detours in mind along the way. Out here, of course, the line is above ground, and you can while away the time by gazing out at the pocket-sized back gardens, some totally neglected and overgrown, some pin-neat, looking ready to be assessed for a Sunday colour magazine competition.

Beyond Acton Town, the District Line stops at all stations, while the parallel Piccadilly Line speeds its Heathrow passengers non-stop past the rural idyll-sounding Turnham Green, Stamford Brook and Ravenscourt Park to Hammersmith.

Within a few hundred yards of Ravenscourt Park station is the national Polish Club, POSK, in King Street. This houses a club, a cultural centre, a hotel and a university. Another university, yes. But there is a good reason for this one. Throughout the years when the Communists ran Poland into the ground, this seat of learning, and others like it round the world, kept Polish knowledge and education and culture alive.

Over a meal in the fully-licensed restaurant, I learned something about the Polish community in Britain. I felt comfortably at home under the crucifix and photograph of the Pope.

I had met the Pope during his 1983 visit to the UK. Indeed, as Lord Lieutenant of Glasgow, I welcomed him to the city. After the formal words of welcome, we exchanged a few words of banter about Scotland's national dress – according to ITN that night, I was the first kilted person that he had met. I turned to introduce him to my wife and family. We have three children. At that time Teresa, the eldest, was a typical, slightly awkward, teenager (she has since blossomed into a beautiful woman, just like her mother) while Mandy and David still retained the cuteness of younger, blond children. Subconsciously, as I realised afterwards, I had pushed the younger two forward. After he had kissed both of them, I said to him 'And this is Teresa.' With the instant perception of the charismatic, he assessed the situation and corrected it beautifully and diplomatically. 'Ah,' said His Holiness, 'she is the first.' She blushed and has never forgotten it. She was the only one of the children that he spoke to.

I like eating, and I like eating ethnic food. The hottest curry doesn't worry me and – just like Joe Baker who left the Edinburgh football club, Hibs, for Turin with the immortal quote – 'I can fair go my pasta'. So, given the opportunity to try Poland's national dishes, after perusing the tongue-twisting titles, I ordered, from the English translations, a selection of specialities.

But it's not just the names that are heavy. Everything about a Polish meal is. *Pierogi Z Nadzieniem Do Wyboro* is dumplings with a choice of fillings. Filling is the word. *Golabki* is cabbage leaves stuffed with minced meat and rice. Stuffed is the word. *Nalesniki Ze Szpinakiem W Sosie Koperkowym* is pancakes packed with spinach in dill sauce. And packed is the word for them.

The food lay on a large silver platter, greasy and steaming and overcooked. Everything slowly slid together. In the mouth, too. The tastes and textures were indistinguishable. The whole congealing mass lay in my stomach for hours. I do not mean to be ungrateful.

At Hammersmith, the District Line plunges into its 'cut and cover mode', just yards below the surface, with the streets above effectively the cover for the train cutting below. This was the method first used to create London's 'underground' railway network, before the technology developed by Brunel allowed the mole-like excavation of the deeper–level Tubes. They obviously forgot to cover Barons Court and West Kensington, which lie forlornly in their open culvert as trains race through to Earl's Court and beyond.

Earl's Court was where Buffalo Bill staged his Wild West Show. Is there anything more incongruous than an Indian chief singing 'There's no Business like Show Business'?

I was to get off at West Brompton. There was another famous London cemetery nearby and I wanted to check a particular grave. Or at least, a monument. It was to a World War I flyer, Sub-Lt Reginald Alexander John Warneford who died shooting down a zeppelin.

It's a long walk from Gloucester Road underground station to the Royal Albert Hall of Arts and Sciences. It's much the same distance from South Kensington, but if you walk it in the company of enthusiastic promenaders, the time flies. You can choose to walk at street level, of course, and that was what I had determined to do, having been promised that it was a fine walk. But there's also a very long and impressive ceramic tile-lined Victorian underground walkway which takes you right up Exhibition Road, avoiding the intervening street crossings. This was the route that I eventually chose.

The passage is livened up by large numbers of colourful posters, and is a kind of art gallery of its own. As I passed the sign to the Natural History Museum, I was tempted to pop in, but thought better of it because I knew I would become so fascinated I would want to stay for hours. I did not have the same feelings as my walk took me past the Science Museum. Even as a boy I had no interest in working working models; and Meccano sets gave me a dull headache. Thank goodness, the graphic designers have taken over. As they always had, in their way, at the Victoria and Albert Museum across the road.

One design element lacking in the subway is a decent litter bin. I had wandered in with my can of diet Tango. There was no place to dispose of it. Certainly the cool, smooth, dry, Devon-stone floor was far too clean to throw it away. Others had solved the problems by perching their empties on the advertising frames. But that looked tacky. So, I carried my can up into the night and threw it among the overflowing 'contents' of the first bin in Exhibition Road.

The bin was directly opposite the Mormon church, with its fairly spectacular floodlit golden spire. An attractive building, it is not on the scale of those granite monoliths in Salt Lake City. The acoustics are so good in Tabernacle Hall, that from the back you can hear a pin drop on the stage. Literally.

The Mormon Church fascinates me. As I understand it, in 1823, this guy, Joseph Smith, found a set of gold plates in New York state, the writing on which, when translated by him, amounted to a new book of the bible, the Book of Mormon. When he had finished the translation the plates, of course, disappeared.

The great attraction of this new religion was that it was uniquely American, the book predicting the discovery of that Continent. If I can remember the lecture in Salt Lake City, the theory was that the lost tribe of Israel boarded a submarine and sailed to America just after the time of Christ. So, America was God's own country.

And so to the Albert Hall. Queen Victoria claimed it reminded her of the British constitution. Said quickly, it sounds witty and profound. Analysis yields no such characteristics. The most ingenious thing about this venerable institution was the innovative way that it was funded. It was Prince Albert who had the idea of a vast cultural and educational campus in Kensington. This came hard on the success of his first great idea, to have a Great Exhibition in 1851 to show off the industrial skills and manufacturing ingenuity of Britain to the world.

While this was a magnificent triumph – it even made a profit – as far as Albert was concerned, it exposed the imbalance between the material superiority which the industrial revolution had given Britain and the world of art and culture. A great hall was therefore to be the catalyst to the promotion of the arts and learning. Albert died before the plans could be properly developed, and the hall was eventually built as a memorial to him.

Despite the wealth associated with the Victorian era, raising the £250,000 needed for the project was as difficult as raising the equivalent sum today would be. Finally, someone hit upon the idea of selling the seats on 999-year leases as the way to bridge the funding gap. Nowadays, all kinds of arenas and stadia go down a similar debenture route.

Today, the Albert Hall is looking for millennium funding to support a nine-year programme costing £57 million. There seems to be so little imagination to many of the millennium submissions. I would much rather that the money is reserved for inspirational *new* projects, not refurbishments or extensions of existing institutions. The Victorians displayed real millennium vision. We seem to be dedicated to catching up on 50 years of past neglect, though the £42 million for a Sutherland-to-Southampton cycle route is altogether more visionary.

The most interesting millennium plans centre around a Globorama at Greenwich, which have that inspirational look. To base the millennium celebration on Greenwich is just right, because that is where it will officially start. Mind you, obsession with the exact second is the great paradox of the century. Because everyone is ignoring the fact that we are counting down to the wrong year. As there is no 'Year Zero' between BC and AD, centuries begin on year '1', 1701, 1801 and 1901. So, 2000 is the one hundredth year of the twentieth century and the new millennium doesn't start until the next year. Why do you think Arthur C. Clark called his book *2001*?

Before the concert, I managed a look behind the scenes at 'the nation's village hall' – so called because of the wide variety of events staged there from classical music concerts to fashion shows, from university graduation ceremonies to military displays. The formula works. The Hall generates a substantial operating surplus.

For a visit to the Albert Hall, you need first to be aware of the statistics. It is about a quarter of the size of the Colosseum in Rome. The long diameter of the outer wall is 272 feet and the shorter, 238 feet. There were six million bricks used in its construction and the basement took 2,000 tons of concrete. The arena is 102 feet by 68 feet, with 1,000 movable chairs. The original total capacity was 5,166: it is now 5,200, but only 3,884 for a concert, with 1,300 'private' seats in the familiar boxes around the periphery.

The part of the Hall that most delighted contemporary critics was the outer balcony. One newspaper remarked: 'Visitors will be allowed to walk and, it is said, gentlemen to smoke, on this balcony.' Not any more they can't.

Like most of show business, the glamour and tinsel is all reserved for the front of house. Backstage is cramped and spartan. Stars are only treated like stars when they are in public view. Impresarios, like journalists, know their common humanity beneath the glitz. And that is how they are treated.

Standing on the stage confirms the vastness of the auditorium. At the same time, you can get some idea of why performers describe it as intimate. The hall is *not* round, but elliptical. The eye follows the 'narrower' sides and makes a circle of them by 'pulling' the far end nearer, making the circumference of the 'circle' seem smaller.

The danger in asking to tour a place like this is that you might be asked to go where you'd rather not – places, for example, of vertiginous height. I got sucked into this one. First I was taken out onto the external balcony which runs round the whole hall, and affords views of the city. No problem so far, as it's not very high by the standards of, say, the nearby Hilton Hotel. From there, an external staircase took me to the roof, still perfectly safe as it is well away from the side of the building. But then I was taken inside again between the two skins of roof. I now had to walk up the curving slope that led up the dome. I was pretty nervous by now, but on I was led out into the middle of the roof to the edge of an open metal grille that covers the 12-foot hole in the middle of the ceiling. I was no longer happy, but was committed now. My guide walked confidently out over the bouncing wire mesh. I waited 'til he came back to safety – I wasn't risking his jumping up and down on it for a laugh – and crept over the gaping holes in the grille right to the middle of the ceiling. I looked down on the red velvet chairs a dizzying 146 feet straight down and felt very sick.

After that, the concert was an anti-climax. But, it was by the Ulster Orchestra. Changed days, the Northern Ireland peace process was in full swing, so there was no need for extra security. Shostakovich, Symphony No 10 in E Minor, with Rachmaninov as an encore.

If you walk the other way from South Kensington station, you enter the area of central London least well served by the Tube, exclusive Chelsea (although, not surprisingly, there are plans for a new Chelsea–Hackney line). The paradox is that Lots Road, south of Battersea Bridge, is the location of the power station that supplies nearly half the energy required to work the Underground system. Incidentally, the height of the Lots Road chimney made it eminently suitable for hanging radio transmission aerials from in the early pre-BBC days of experimental broadcasts in the 1920s. But most of Chelsea is much less utilitarian.

I decided to board the District Line again at West Brompton, which was the terminus of the first southern extension of this line in 1869, and headed southwards for a spot of tennis. To get to Wimbledon, you actually get off at Southfields, opened by the London and South Western Railway in 1889.

Wimbledon, SW19, is one of London's better suburbs, with expensive middle-class housing. An enterprising lot. Because, despite the tens of thousands that they must earn to afford to live here, many of the residents of Wimbledon Park Road supplement their incomes by letting out their driveways as car parking spaces for the two weeks in June/July when the All-England championships take place. At £9 a time and room for half a dozen cars in many gardens, the Wimbledon fortnight is a nice little earner. And it doesn't stop at parking. They also rent the entrances to their gardens to souvenir stall-holders. They were selling everything from tee-shirts to Holey Bagels! A side of Wimbledon ruthlessly suppressed by Dan Maskell. Oh, I say!

If this was a shock, it was nothing to the horror I felt when I saw what they were doing to the golf course in Wimbledon Park. They were parking cars on it! Thousands of them, stretched from tee to roped-off green as live commentary was piped to them from speakers suspended from the trees. All these years, tennis has conveyed an innocent, naïve, simple, genuine image of Corinthian enthusiasm for the game, which has concealed the sporting vandal lurking beneath.

And they had no need to use their cars. There were plenty of extra trains (which must make the Underground a fortune). These linked up with an integrated shuttle bus or a system of shared taxis which made the transport arrangements much better than at Lord's.

The pavement outside the All-England Club looked like the dockside at Pireaus during a ferry strike. A tented village had sprung up, inhabited by young people of all nationalities camping out.

At Lord's, I noticed how television can make many events seem more imposing than they really are. It has had the opposite effect on Wimbledon. The buildings of the club look more venerable in reality and the ivy thicker. Those were my first impressions, as I arrived on my first-ever visit to the All-England Club which I felt I knew so well from my annual trips through the box.

I arrived rather late in the day, too late even to explore the possibility of buying a ticket. So I just walked in. And nobody challenged me. The first thing that I did was buy the strawberries and cream. Even at £1.75, they were delicious. I then wandered up, through crowds that were much thicker than I expected, to have a look at Number One Court, where a mixed doubles game was in progress. It was easy enough to get up to the stand level, but at every entrance from the passageway into the seat there was a security guard. Or rather a service person. It seems that every year Wimbledon can secure the exclusive services of the British Armed Forces to patrol the championships. Who pays for it all, I wondered? Or is it regarded as in-house training to prepare soldiers for careers as commissionaires?

I managed briefly to elude capture, and stood looking out over the court. Another surprise. The baseline, which looks so long on telly, is just the same size as my local tennis club. When I went on to look out over a deserted Centre Court, the smallness of the playing area was reinforced. This contrasted with the vastness of the stands. Television gives only an indication of how big these really are. They are the size of football stands – and better appointed.

Even the outer courts have, in the main, plenty of seats. And are extremely well maintained. This is a very impressive sporting complex.

I walked back through the owner-occupying stall-holders and carried on to the end of the line at Wimbledon. At Ealing, I had already noticed the cathedral-like bank. Here they have a church that serves as the local branch of Boots!

Calling the big mall which dominates the station the Centre Court Shopping Centre, this far from the tennis, is cheating a bit. But everyone was getting in on this great marketing opportunity. Even the YMCA were offering strawberries and cream during Wimbledon week – and for 75p less than at . . . well, Wimbledon.

The District Line has the distinction of serving more stations than any other on the London Underground system – 60 in all, over a route extending over 40 miles. Much of the line's infrastructure is well over 100 years old, and there's an ongoing but none-too-urgent programme of refurbishment.

Probably they're right to resist the temptation to destroy what is a unique collection of conspicuous heritage. The variety of station architecture, for example, forms a time capsule of styling and reflects the historical development of the line. It's one thing for deep-level Tube stations to be given the modern designer-tile veneer treatment in lining their basic cylindrical form. It's quite another to homogenise the interesting street–level architecture of previous generations. So let's revel in the District Line's many curious little stations.

Upminster, in the silliest-named of all the London boroughs, Havering, is at the eastern end of the District Line.

The trip out was one of the dreariest made. The marshy Essex landscape starts off being depressing, a characteristic that the industrial and cheap housing development sets out to complement.

I found little of interest on the way out. There was a sign on a house in East Ham – 'If you lived here you would be home by now'. Passing through a place with another silly name, Barking, I could see a mosque poking up between the renovated multi-storeys. I'm not yet politically-correct enough not to find this surprising. Not so much exotic as intrusive. Dagenham Heathway is marked 'for the Ford works'. The sign is an old one done in the old style Ford logo. I would have expected an international company like Ford to put much more effort into its corporate image. Maybe if I had got off the train I would have seen some evidence of this.

The marsh between Dagenham East and Elm Park didn't cheer me up any. But the appearance of Dagenham again reminded me of the other institution for which it is, or was, famous – the Dagenham Girl Pipers. Every so often they would appear on the television screen of my childhood, and disappear again. They were never then billed as the 'Band that Hitler Loved', but they could have because they had played for him, outside the Reichchancellery in 1937. He is said to have enjoyed it very much.

However, 'the story of Dagenham's Piping Ambassadors unfolds itself as a once-in-a-lifetime romance which, right from the commencement of its opening chapter, holds the interest and grips the imagination' according to the official history. The band was started in 1930 by the Rev. J. W. Graves, Dagenham's first Congregational minister. He appointed Pipe-Major G. Douglas Taylor of the King's Own Scottish Borderers as their first tutor. The KOSB was due for amalgamation with the Royal Scots until a public outcry in Scotland saved them. There are now only 600 of them left, and there may well be rather more Dagenham Girl Pipers!

You have to admire the single-minded way in which Graves went about the creation of this curious institution. The girls were taught and practised in secret for 18 months before their first concert – the audience for which consisted entirely of newspaper reporters. The next day, more than 100 newspapers told the unusual story. The Rev. Graves missed his vocation: he would have been brilliant in PR.

Slightly old-fashioned, the organisation continues today unfazed by such things as equal opportunities legislation. Boys are not allowed to join. Neither are girls – unless they live in Dagenham. The band, I was told, do not participate in any of the piping competitions organised in Scotland, 'as we have nothing to prove'.

I wasn't expecting too much of Upminster so the windmill was a pleasant surprise. It springs into view behind the trees just as you approach the station. It is a timber smock mill, built in 1803 to meet the demand for home-produced flour during the Napoleonic Wars. It was acquired by Essex County Council in 1937. They wanted to demolish it and build houses on the site. But a local outcry saved it, and it now stands restored to full working order in an open field.

There has been a settlement at Upminster at least since Roman times. But, despite this long history, there is very little of interest to record – the archetypal influence of Essex man. It hasn't even been a place that has produced famous people. The best known is probably Sir James Wedgwood Benn MP, grandfather of Tony.

Coming back city-ward, as we approached Bromley-by-Bow, I spotted a couple of what looked to my untutored eye like oast-houses beside an interesting-looking clock tower. I just had to have a look.

The road outside Bromley-by-Bow station is the approach to the Blackwall Tunnel. It's so busy that the central divider has an extra fence built on top to take it above head-height. But the underpass provided me with the route to the other side, where I went in search of the London Gas Museum. The search was not encouraging. I knew from the map that it was there, but all I could find was the entrance to a gasworks. I decided to hazard a question to the security guard.

'What's your name? None?' he asked. It must be the effects of the gas.

'I'm sorry. I don't follow you,' I mumbled, hoping that was near enough to the correct answer.

'Nunn. Are you the Mr Nunn that has an appointment?' he insisted.

'No, no. You mean I need an appointment?' And that was the end of that.

Well, I wasn't about to try and argue my way into a gas museum. But I would have liked to have walked on the site. Because here, although there is no sign of it now, there once stood the munitions factory founded by William Congreve. His new rockets had earlier been used in the 1812 war against America. This was the war that the United States declared when Britain was having a little local difficulty with Napoleon, but which the British, nonetheless, won. The rockets were brought to bear in the attack on Baltimore's Fort McHenry where their noise kept a certain Francis Scott Key off his sleep. He passed the night writing about them;

And the rockets' red glare, the bombs bursting in air,
Gave proof through the night that our flag was still there.

And the United States had a new national anthem, although it wasn't officially recognised as such until 1930.

Instead, I turned to look for the way to the clock tower. I had stumbled quite by accident on an area redolent in the economic history of London. The area roughly bounded by the Tube stations at Bromley, West Ham, Stratford and Mile End is a reminder of the almost infinite variety of facets that combine as a great city develops. Though the Romans were here, this is not Roman London.

125

It is not the sophisticated London that Dr Johnson never tired of. It is not the great international financial capital. It is not the political heart of what was once a great empire. This is the bread-and-butter London of the essential trades. The London that had to develop to feed, water and supply the population. The London which suffered industrial despoilation as a result.

The old mill is located at a fairly complicated piece of waterway which includes the River Lee, or Lea, as it is sometimes spelt, before it runs into Bow Creek. And the economic fortunes of the area were tied to the river.

On this small tributary, Caesar fought the Britons and Alfred dammed the Danes. In 1424, the Lee was the first river in England that interested Parliament sufficiently for legislation to be passed to allow for the improvement of its navigation. Grain for food had to be kept flowing from the country to the city, and Parliament ensured that improvement continued to be made over the centuries.

The towers I had spotted are, in fact, grain-drying kilns, one of the more recent additions dating from around 1800. The mills themselves go back to before the Norman Conquest. In the fourteenth century, Edward III, an unashamed interventionist, had targeted the area for economic expansion. As a result, a lot of smelly and dangerous industries, like bone boiling for soap, calico printing, tanning, and gunpowder making, unwelcome in the city of London, were established. Even nowadays, it occurred to me, the nearest nuclear power station to London is even further downwind – 50 miles away at Bradwell in Essex.

In 1588, the Three Mills area comprised two water-mills, one for corn and one for gunpowder. No one seems to know where the third mill went to, or came from. A couple of decades later, soldiers returning from another of the interminable European wars of the period, brought back with them a new drink, called in Dutch 'jenever', which the English shortened to 'gin' and adopted as their national drink. The mills diversified into exploiting this new fashion.

Some of the milling machinery still remains. The mills around here were originally tidal. These ones here became undershot. Tidal water was collected in a mill pond and then released to drive the mill-wheels from below.

In the nineteenth century, the area became the centre of some

126

pretty foul industries. Apart from the gasworks, a large number of chemical works grew up to avoid restrictions imposed in the city. These places used some fairly disgusting and fundamental raw material – like blood from slaughterhouses from which they manufactured fertiliser.

In nearby Bow there is a nice block of flats that used to be the Fairfield Bryant and May match factory. Discontent among the workers there in 1880 led to the formation of the first ever women's trade union, the Union of Women Matchmakers – and the famous matchgirls' strike in 1888.

All of this industrial development inevitably produced more than its share of pollution. When the authorities got round to doing something about it in the middle of the nineteenth century, they built the Northern Outfall Sewer and a pumping station at Stratford. This building, which can be seen from the Tube at West Ham, was designed by Joseph Bazalgette, who later worked on the Thames Embankment and the District Line and was known as 'Mr Underground'.

The red brick building is detailed with elaborate stonework and bands of blue brick in a curious mixture of Italian and Gothic styles. Its cruciform plan caused it to be dubbed the Cathedral of Sewage, although if its original two Moorish chimneys had been still standing it would pass as a mosque. Sadly, they proved too good a landmark for the Luftwaffe and were demolished during the war.

The Northern Outfall Sewer Embankment, appropriately foreshortened to NOSE, is now a four-and-a-half-mile long landscaped footpath from Bow to Beckton. In fact, the whole of the Lee Valley, at least the 20 miles from rural Hertfordshire right in to the East End here, has been looked after since 1967 by a regional park authority charged with regeneration. When I was there, although the work has hardly begun on this part of the project, people were sunbathing and fishing.

Stepping out from Whitechapel station, you step into what many people might say is the real London. If it wasn't for the noise of the traffic you could hear the sound of Bow bells from here – that is, if they hadn't been destroyed during the wartime bombing.

This was a tough part of town. In the eighteenth century many anti-social industries like brick–making and brewing were located here, downwind of the dwellings of the wealthy. The nearby docks have continuously disgorged boatloads of immigrants from the time of the Huguenots around 1685.

It was in the wide Whitechapel Road that the Jewish Socialist Club used to meet. In 1907, it played host to the Fifth Congress of the Russian Social Democratic Labour Party. All the criminals who established the Soviet Union were there – Stalin, Lenin and Trotsky included. Here, they were introduced to a wealthy American, George Fels, who was daft enough to lend them £1,700 (worth about £70,000 today) to help finance the revolution. It is said that they paid him back. History does not record if they paid interest.

This was also the beat of a slightly less notorious murderer, Jack the Ripper, whose extravagances were on a much smaller scale than Stalin's. Between August and November 1888, six prostitutes were murdered in Whitechapel and Aldgate. The crimes sent shock waves through London and the police and Home Secretary were roundly criticised for failing to catch the killer. Their failure led to a riot of endless speculation as to who could have been responsible. Among the more bizarre theories was that the Prince of Wales had been the murderer. To this day the mysteries have not been solved.

The East End is doing its very best to drag itself up by its bootstraps. But it hasn't succeeded yet. The local boroughs, and the East End Tourism Trust, have churned out brochures which make the place look as good as Glasgow's Merchant City. But the reality is disappointing.

The promise is of cheery Cockneys and ethnic interest. But this is a poor, run-down area. The difference between the politically-correct local politicians and their electorate is written on the entrances to the East London Mosque – one for 'men' and one for 'ladies'.

The new houses in Brick Lane are brick. And the street signs are in English and Urdu. Surely a retrograde step. The temperature of America's melting pot was maintained by insisting that everyone speak English. That is breaking down, as Spanish now dominates in large parts of Florida and California. The quicker immigrants lose their accents the better – including Scots! Although ambiguous shop signs like 'Bangladeshi fish' can still force a smile.

Spitalfield Market brought me back to more familiar territory –
the theme parking of Great Britain. This fruit and vegetable market,
founded in 1682, shut a few years ago to be redeveloped as a leisure
shopping area. But the money ran out, and it sits unfinished. I
enjoyed a delicious coffee and a chocolate croissant in the temporary
little café. But there was no East End bustle around me. There was a
sign advertising Britain's first organic food market, but that was only
on Fridays and Sundays. And the craft shops were shut.

I walked along Brushfield Street, which runs down the side of the
market, and burst into Bishopsgate. 'Burst' was how it felt, because
the change in atmosphere was immediate and dramatic. Here in front
of me was the power and wealth of the City. Behind me was the
dowdiness and decay of the workers.

The impressive new glass and marble building at 155 Bishopsgate
soared upwards in the direction of the great god Mammon. It seemed
familiar to me . . . I'd seen it on television, I was sure . . . ah yes,
Barings Bank. It still looks good despite blowing £850 million on a
day's gambling.

Walking on down Bishopsgate to Middlesex Street, which today
was not masquerading as Petticoat Lane, I made my way back to
Aldgate East and resumed my travels. The station there had the most
inept slogan that I had seen on the Underground.

This was entirely out of character because London Underground
prides itself on its witty advertising. Slogans such as 'Go, Van,
Gogh', which was used to promote travel to museums and
exhibitions, display wit and creativity. This quality was recognised
by American Bill Apfelbaum when London Transport Advertising
Ltd was privatised.

In 1989, Apfelbaum, a graduate of New York University in
Manhattan, and advertising veteran at New York Subways
Advertising, took over the reigns at an old established company
which dominates the transport advertising in the Big Apple and 25
major markets across the US. From then he dreamed of acquiring the
franchise to handle transport advertising in London, which he
recognised as 'transit heaven', the best in the world. So, when the
chance came in 1994, he wasted no time in acquiring London
Transport Advertising.

TDI quickly built on its London presence and doubled its UK

business from transport advertising within the next 18 months, with contract gains on bus fleets throughout the UK. In Ireland, TDI won advertising on bus, rail and roadside posters. Advertisers including fashion houses, film distributors and retailers have all rallied to TDI, which now delivers campaigns simultaneously from London to Leeds, Dumfries to Dublin. I rang Bill Apfelbaum's office in the States. 'London's Underground is the jewel in the crown of transport advertising. Not only is it a comprehensive and wonderful transport system but the facility provides an unmatched environment for advertisers. It seems the creators of the ads are aware of where their work is being placed, as it so often hits the spot.'

CHAPTER SEVEN

ELEMENTARY, MY LORD BUCKINGHAM

The driving force behind the Bakerloo Line was the anxiety of a few businessmen in the City of London to get to Lord's in time to see the last hour of Test match play without having to leave their offices too early. Exactly the kind of criterion that should be used in investment decisions!

Once they had determined their priorities, it was a simple step to overcome the previously grave funding problems which the scheme had encountered since 1865. In 1891, a Bill was promoted in Parliament to allow the tunnels to be dug. But, despite the lure of the cricket, the line was not opened until the next century.

In the end, when the Bakerloo Line did open in 1906 it was, ironically, American money which made it possible. It took its original name from the stations between which the railway was first planned, Baker Street and Waterloo. But, very quickly, a popular evening newspaper collapsed it to 'Bakerloo'.

I intended to start my journey at one end of the original line, Baker Street. But before going in, I searched among the scaffolding which covered most of the station building for the Chiltern Court restaurant that Betjeman enjoyed so much. But it seems to have gone. Chiltern Court is there, exclusive apartments with a forbidding doorman, but not the restaurant. The nearest was a Burger King across the road, but I'm sure Betjeman would not have eulogised that.

Baker Street is one of the oldest parts of the whole system. The lift doors are in brass, like those of a five-star hotel. There are clean, unbroken, brown and white tiles all the way to these lifts. It was the only station where I felt compelled to spend some time, because it does manage to impart a sense of history. It combines the new for the Bakerloo and Metropolitan Lines with a hint of the old as you walk down a short flight of stairs to join the Circle Line. This takes you under an old metal arch where the destinations are described in black letters on white.

Baker Street station features several times in Sir Arthur Conan Doyle's stories. Not surprisingly, as Sherlock Holmes lived in Baker Street itself. Every schoolboy knows that his address was 221B. But where exactly is that?

If you were to write to Sherlock Holmes – and, believe it or not, 200 people do every year and from all over the world – the Post Office will deliver your letter to the Abbey National Building Society, because their address covers the vital number. For the past 60 years, the society has employed a member of staff as Sherlock Holmes's secretary, to answer the letters. But the mystery doesn't end there because, strangely enough, there are two 221B addresses in Baker Street. The second number is outside the Sherlock Holmes Museum – which is a proper flat, not an office – which has been designed as a faithful reproduction of Holmes's lodgings as described by his Scottish creator. The Post Office refused to deliver letters to the Great Dectective here, arguing that it was not the address. So the Museum solved the problem by nipping out and forming a company called 221B Ltd. So their sign isn't an address. It's a company name. Elementary.

The 1995 Bakerloo train that arrived to pick me up at Baker Street was bright and modern, painted in red, white and blue. I was looking for one to take me all the way to Harrow and Wealdstone, but all three posted on the indicator board were to stop short – at Queen's Park. So I decided to take the first one that came along, rather than wait for one that went all the way.

I discovered later that Queen's Park was the first terminus of the northern extension completed in 1915, which was then extended again to Watford Junction in 1917. Ironically, in 1982, the service to Watford was withdrawn and Queen's Park became the terminus once again. But only for a few more years, as customer demand forced the re-opening of the service as far as Harrow and Wealdstone in 1989. The line had to be kept operational anyway, because the main depot of the Bakerloo Line is at Stonebridge Park, which is beyond Queen's Park.

The first part of the journey reeks of the Monopoly board.

Marylebone High Street is one of the four stations on the British version of the evergreen board game. It's been many years since Marylebone was a major force in the railway system, and I often wonder why the designers of the game chose it. Maybe the American inventor just liked the English eccentricity of the name, which is, of course, French. But it isn't the only odd choice. Fenchurch Street station is another. But surely the most cursory inspection of the map of Central London would suggest that either Shaftesbury Avenue or Haymarket are more important than nearby Coventry Street? And why tiny Vine Street?

Paddington is not on the Monopoly circuit, but it is one of the great railway stations of the world, redolent of the Victorian age of railway engineering achievement. As the main terminus for train journeys to and from Wales and the West Country, it reeks of Isambard Kingdom Brunel and his kind – heroic figures whose contribution to the infrastructure of Britain is still under-acknowledged.

If Brunel's time had been plagued with the kind of civil disobedience environmental protest groups we suffer from today, the railways of Britain would never have been constructed – including those within the London Underground system. Can you imagine the fury which would nowadays greet plans to scythe through the countryside with embankments and cuttings, or to straddle roads with high level bridges, or to 'cut and cover' under busy streets? I'm all for being sensitive about the environment in such matters, but architects and engineers should be credited with some kind of social conscience. Nowadays, you can rely on protesters appearing like flies in the summer time when someone wants to build something. Different protesters swarm round again decades or centuries later, when someone else wants to take it down!

Warwick Avenue, at first sight, is a place that could be taken down without even the scruffiest protester protesting. Not that it's tacky or dirty, just bland, and characterless – an undistinguished area of upmarket flats and office premises. Right across from the station is a peculiar looking church, the Church of St Saviour. The brick building itself is OK, I suppose. What is odd is the ugly metal spire. Because of the small surrounding buildings it looks tall and – unfortunately, because it really isn't nice – it draws attention to itself.

I haven't seen many canals, but the Regent's Canal is the first one I've seen with an island in it. It's even big enough to have a name. It's called after the poet, Browning. Yes, I've been to Venice, but the islands there are in the lagoon, not the canals. The name of this area, Little Venice, is a misnomer. This is nothing like Venice. For one thing it doesn't smell. For another it doesn't have the architecture or that marvellous feel of decaying grandeur. But, in a very different way from Venice, it is a beautiful spot and deserves a name of its own. I propose London Lagoon.

I walked past the barges converted to art galleries, restaurants, cafés or homes to a bridge made in 1900 from iron and red sandstone. From here, you can look into a picturesque canal office. It was Sunday and the roads were quiet. Indeed, I walked down the middle of Old Blomfield Road without being disturbed to the Paddington Stop public house. There a new man had brought his infant daughter to drink with his pals. But he was having the usual success that men have in stopping her crying.

Just on the curve of the canal beyond the pub were some modern flats. I was astonished to discover that they were part of the Amberley council estate. Further into the estate away from the canal, the houses looked like any other council houses with signs of neglect and damage. But the ones on the canal front were in great condition and were being looked after, as the carefully-tended window boxes indicated.

I walked back to the station up Formosa Street and Bristol Gardens. Number 29 had the most unusual door-stop – a three-foot-high bomb with fins painted white. I longed to knock on the door to find out the story. But I decided that people who keep a bomb at their front door are maybe not the best people to disturb, but you can ask them if you like.

Maida Vale was my next stop-off. The only thing that registered in my mind about the name was that it was where much of the BBC's classical music programmes were produced. Very Third Programme. Very Radio Three. From the map, I had discovered a Lanark Road with three prominently marked buildings, Edinburgh House, Falkirk House and Glasgow House. The map showed them as large and impressive. I was intrigued, having never heard of them. Were they records buildings of some kind? I determined to find out.

The station at Maida Vale is old-fashioned and carefully preserved. Its wall tiles and cast-iron are evident reminders of its Victorian influences – though the station wasn't opened until 1915.

Maida Vale itself is a street . . . classy, leafy – and, for a Scotsman, redolent of home. There are plenty of Scottish connections – indeed, much of the decorative cast-iron was probably from Glasgow, which was a major centre for this kind of architectural ironwork. Elgin Mews is classic upper-class London. The houses looked expensive, But, surprisingly, the cars in the converted stables were very ordinary – a Micra, a Metro and one dusty, C-registered BMW.

'Mews' to me was a word associated with superior London, an image strengthened by the countless cinema portrayals. I am thinking particularly of the TV version of *The Saint*, Leslie Charteris's Bayswater villain, whose smart Swedish sports car seemed always to be sweeping in and out of 'mews'. The connection, I assumed, was that earlier form of transport, the horse. Mews were stables converted to luxury flats. Not so. Long before they saw a horse mews were buildings where birds of prey were kept to mew, or molt. It wasn't until about 1490 that horses were first kept in the Royal Mews by Henry VII. Now that I know that, I can never look a mews in the eye again.

Through Elgin Mews with my eyes shut and on to Lanark Road – and there were the three buildings. They were 17-storey council housing tower blocks. Despite their recent vintage, they had been even more recently renovated. Edinburgh was beige, Falkirk red and Glasgow (from the Gaelic for 'dear, green place'), accurately, green. Inside, there was a plastic mural (damaged). On the floor, recently renovated rubber tiles were already missing.

To recover from this acute disappointment, I went into a little fenced-off area of grass, not worthy of the name park, and sat down. Already there were two old ladies sitting in the cheap plastic, tubular legs-type of deck-chairs. As I walked past, one looked up and quickly looked down at her handbag to make sure it was safe and kept her hand on it until I left. I wonder what other measures she would have been driven to if she had heard my accent. An old Mark X Jag was sitting in the car park, its sleek looks disguising insurmountable operational problems. The council houses are very often the opposite. Despite the best attempts of architects to make

135

them uninviting and uninhabitable the better tenants manage to make them work against the odds.

On the opposite side of the road were more modern council houses – of the *Play School* shape, but with basements and outdoor stairs at the side. Opened in 1982, they showed that the municipalities had at least learned some lessons that housing for the masses is not the same as mass housing.

After Kilburn Park, the line emerges into the open air, and rumbles on to Queen's Park. I went out into Harvist Road and down to Kilburn police station. Is this where IRA terrorists are held for questioning? If so, why? A long wait at Queen's Park station was explained to me by the impersonal voice of the tannoy as being caused by a broken rail at Watford. Well it would, wouldn't it?

As soon as I got on the train, I was confronted by not one but an extraordinary three Underground inspectors. One – a woman of impressive girth – asked for my ticket. After a cursory search, it was clear that I was going to have trouble finding it. So two of the inspectors left to go into the next carriage, leaving the third – a man – to deal with me. I searched everywhere two or three times but, embarrassingly, I could not find it. I pulled a set of business cards from my top pocket and rummaged through them.

'I hope you haven't been using these,' laughed the inspector.

I gave up. He indicated that he would have to charge me the single fare from Heathrow to Harrow. He was obviously using his discretion not to charge me the £10 penalty.

He sat down to write out the ticket. Just then, one final scrabble through my satchel produced the ticket.

'I was determined to find it so that you would believe that I bought one,' I said.

'Oh, I never doubt a customer's word,' he replied.

He seemed more human than the average Gestapo *Obergruppenfuerher*, so I attempted a conversation. He had been a probation officer. This job paid more.

'Without giving anything away,' he said, 'my basic is in the high twenties. With overtime and so on I can get it up to thirty-four thousand pounds a year. A train driver's basic is twenty-three. 'I like the variety,' he went on. 'I do other types of fraud as well – for example, checking on the people who sell the tickets. We are trained in accountancy and law.... not just Underground law, but civil law, so we know what people's civil rights are.'

Was he trained in dealing with customers? 'Not really. I got that from my previous job.' It's some society that pays ticket inspectors more than probation officers, I thought.

And I was so harassed by this experience that I stayed on the train all the way to the terminus. I'd been to Harrow proper on the Metropolitan Line, and visited the school. In its wider sense, Harrow is, of course, a London borough and like all the rest announces this on its signs. But Harrow is different. It defines itself as 'a *responsible* London borough' – implicitly criticising those who are not. Presumably those like Brent next door.

At Harrow and Wealdstone, you have a choice. If you walk straight out of the station, you are in Harrow. If you cross over the bridge, you come out in Wealdstone. The station itself is of the old-fashioned British Rail type with wooden buildings and a wood-clad bridge. The Harrow exit takes you into a car park and on to a suburban back street. There are signs to the Civic Centre and the Magistrates Court, which I followed until another Seventies office block came into view – not the type of place that I would associate with representing the burghers of such a historic place. So I turned back.

The Wealdstone side was marginally more interesting, leading to a busy high street. But it lacked any pretence at affluence and in truth was pretty dreary.

I walked up Masons Avenue onto the road bridge back to Harrow and looked into the Railway Hotel. Of the hotel division of the business there was very little evidence, although someone had hung their laundry out on the flat roof. This was a pub in the grimmest and grimiest sense. There were three bars, Lounge, Public and Food. And a sign announced that all three were open all day. I passed through the peeling door, under the statutory notice indicating that the landlords, or licensees, were Brendan Francis Hipwell and Robert Dermot Hipwell. The Irish character of the place was confirmed by a framed poster of Dublin's millennium. In Scotland or Northern Ireland, I reflected, you would never find a Catholic pub in Masons Avenue.

The unpainted theme that I had noticed outside the Railway Hotel was continued within. There was a dark brown dado running all the way round the room that was the main lounge bar. Harsh wooden chairs failed to entice me to sit down, and severe tables were laid out formally. In the toilet, there were flies and loose tiles to complete the picture.

The decorative themes seemed confused. As well as the Dublin poster there was a series of what looked like cigarette cards with a railway theme. And there was a clock with the legend 'Glasgow Paddle Ship Company'.

The landlord himself was drinking with his customers (a soft drink, I'm sure). He had a lank mop of dirty grey hair which he kept brushing out of his eyes with the hand which permanently held a cigarette. To escape the smoke, I moved into the Food Bar, which was really just a part of the same room, though down a short flight of stairs. I read the menu a couple of times. But the look of the place caused me to lose my appetite, so I left. The customer, they say, is king. Even if the landlord's a republican.

Back at the station, I sat waiting for the train back to town. It was clearly not an Underground station, but a main-line one. The Inter-City trains thundering through rather gave the game away. Returning to the Tube platform, there was a notice: 'This section is owned by British Rail whose single and return fares apply.' My inspector had said nothing of this. The track certainly seemed to make the journey bumpier. Indeed, the line beyond Harrow and Wealdstone to Watford Junction was until 1982 also part of the Underground system, but seems to have been pushed between pillar and post, with British Rail's Network South-East currently in control.

On the return journey I stopped off at Willesden Junction to have a look at the car-breaker's yard that was so clearly marked on the map. I walked past the lines of brick houses that looked like a miners' row. Now restored, they had a cared-for look. One resident had an ingenious window frame which allowed him to grow tomatoes on the second storey. But, although I stood on a rubbish bin to peer over a wall, I could not find the breaker's yard.

Back at the station, I saw that some patriotic person was flying a blue, yellow and red flag in a garden opposite. It was not one I could identify. A man who boarded with me was wearing a hand-knitted, woollen head covering to keep in his dreadlocks: it had the green, yellow and red trim of the Caribbean. It made me wonder whether the green on the flag had faded to blue.

I was still pondering the ticket inspector's story and the unequal and unfair ways in which rewards are distributed in our society when I alighted at Kensal Green and found myself confronted with the evidence of something far more important – life, and death, itself. Directly across Harrow Road coming out of the station is the final resting place of William Makepeace Thackeray, the author of the oft–filmed and televised *Vanity Fair*, which itself is a romance about human behaviour and attitudes in an unequal society.

Kensal Green cemetery was 56 acres of sheep pasture when, following a cholera epidemic in 1832, Parliament licensed its use as a privately owned burial ground, where both Anglicans and non-Anglicans could be laid to rest. It was designed to overcome resistance to being buried in unconsecrated locations, and to provide an alternative to the dangerous and malodorous overcrowding of churchyards, which had led Charles Dickens to moan that 'rot and mildew and dead citizens formed the uppermost scent in the city'.

Like other cemeteries of its era, Kensal Green is full of the most outrageously extravagant mausoleums, designed to impress succeeding generations with the importance of their inhabitants. One of them, which apparently cost £3,000 in 1837 (multiply that by 50 at least to get today's value), commemorates a circus owner, Andrew Ducrow. Its decorative adornments in stone include a sphinx, angels, maidens, a beehive, and sundry mock-ruined columns overgrown with carved wreaths and roses. Don't ask me why there aren't elephants, lions and clowns as well.

I preferred the inscription on a nearby gravestone to a patent medicine merchant: 'He is now at rest and far beyond the praises or censures of this world.' The man obviously had a fairly turbulent relationship with his patients.

Apart from Thackeray's last remains, Kensal Green cemetery also boasts a few other human literary relics – those of William Wilkie Collins, whose best-known work, a Gothic thriller called *The Moonstone*, was not a set book in my schooldays so I know it only from the television adaptation; Anthony Trollope of *Barchester Towers*, the *Brookside* of its time, and many others.

Parliament's intention to provide non-sectarian places for

interment was obviously not welcomed by some non-Anglicans, for on an adjacent site sharing the same entrance is another one – St Mary's Roman Catholic cemetry. Here, though, there is a wonderful human tale to be told – that of Mary Seacole, whose grave is quite inadequate to the stature of this heroine. She was born into Jamaican slave society, but managed to escape from all that, to become one of the first black women in the western world's medical profession. Described as a 'doctress', she was a notable figure in the Crimean War, disgracefully overlooked by those who instead promoted the heroic deeds of Florence Nightingale. Her autobiography, *The Wonderful Adventures of Mrs Seacole in Many Lands*, was published in 1857.

Cemeteries are not my favourite places, but I felt it my duty to look further, especially as I hadn't yet located the graves of Blondin, the tightrope walker, or British General James Barry, a senior army medical officer, who, it was discovered as the body was being prepared for burial, turned out to be another woman doctor. Nor had I found the tomb of Isambard Kingdom Brunel, whose engineering genius had made such a contribution to the early development of the Underground. A workman cutting wood to repair the ceiling stood outside the little chapel. We exchanged greetings. As I walked away, I thought to ask him if he knew where any of these graves were. I turned to talk to him again. But, like all characters in good graveyard stories, he had disappeared. I was glad it was mid-afternoon.

An unlikely hawk, perching on an ornate tombstone, flew off as I approached. The ornate grave, that of Luisa Fowke, who had been born in the 'Empire of Brazil' and died in London in 1890, made me realise the significant difference between the gravestones in the Protestant and Catholic cemeteries. The Catholic one was full of statues of Our Lady of Lourdes and, particularly, the Sacred Heart. In other words, it concentrated on the supernatural, the hereafter. It was looking forward.

In the Protestant reserve, while there were angels and crosses, they were that much more impersonal. There was also an abundance of urns and mourning humans and hearts and obelisks. Life after death was playing a much less significant role here. It was the person's life that was being recognised, and the horror and the loss of death. The contrast between hope and experience.

The map showed that the cemeteries almost backed on to the breaker's yard. I had hoped to catch a glimpse of it to compare the two kinds of dying. But it must have gone.

Mind you, the area itself was doing a fair impersonation of death. I walked back to the station passed a closed garage with a clapped–out Volvo sitting forlornly outside. The hospitality proposed by the Mason's Arms failed to convince me, sitting as it is in the shadow of a derelict office block.

Kensal Green station ranks with the worst. It has new, stark, steel roofs along both platforms and up to cover the stairs that lead to a small, soulless booking hall. There is no information about the trains. The whole thing looks like it has been built for defence.

The southern end of the Bakerloo Line is at the Elephant and Castle – another pub. The elephant is self-explanatory, but there might still be some people who do not know that the castle is the houda, the little house on top of the elephant in which people can travel. The pub name is a relic of British India.

But that is about as romantic as this terminus gets. Outside the station is a large covered shopping centre whose logo is a pink elephant. But, although the centre is laid out in the normal American mall fashion with a lot of fast food outlets, the quality of the shops is poor and the restaurants are not enticing. The rest of the area is just one giant traffic roundabout.

Lambeth North is a move upmarket, though you wouldn't think so at first, spilling out into a confusion of streets. But, once I had sorted my way through the back streets and on to Lambeth Palace Road, the difference was tangible. Lambeth Palace has been the official residence of the Archbishop of Canterbury for seven hundred years.

A few hundred yards upstream, with a commanding view of the Thames, is the building in which Jeffrey Archer, the novelist, lives. For the past seven years he has shared the penthouse with his magnificent collection of modern Scottish paintings. Both the novelist and the churchman can look across the river to the Houses of Parliament, of whose Upper Chamber they are both members, the Archbishop *ex officio*, the writer by his energy. Close by the Archer residence are the new headquarters of MI6, an ostentatiously modern, green and white building which draws attention to itself. Even in these days of open government this seems to be taking things a bit too far. Or is it all a double bluff to allow George Smiley, Harry Palmer and their chums to continue to conduct their nefarious business undisturbed in much less obtrusive surroundings?

I walked the other way, back past St Thomas's Hospital. This centre of medical excellence is so affected by market forces that it feels obliged to sloganise. 'Caring for the community 24 hours a day' or some such words are plastered across the building. Who would believe otherwise?

An integral part of the hospital, the Florence Nightingale Museum is all sparkling white tiles – and that's just on the outside. I glanced inside, ignoring the silly grinning caricature of the founder of modern nursing that serves as the museum's logo, to see a painting of her on the steps of the hospital at Sebastapol. It gave a hint of the bloody and gruesome sights that might be in store. My stomach already weakening, I turned away.

Walking back along Lambeth Palace Road, I could see the Houses of Parliament across the river. And surely that wasn't a sign on the tall block further towards the horizon proclaiming 'University of North London'? I walked on to Westminster Bridge past the old County Hall. Now that London no longer has a council to run it, for the first time since the reign of Richard the Lionheart, the building has been sold to the Japanese and, according to the hoardings, is being converted into 'London's First World-Class Aquarium' and another leisure attraction called Family World. I shivered at the thought of what had brought this fine building to such a fate.

You cannot cross Westminster Bridge without thinking about Wordsworth's poem. But it's not the same bridge as he stood on, and the city has changed dramatically in almost 200 years. Despite which, the river does bestow a tranquillity, and the 'towers, domes, theatres and temples' are still there. It was morning, early, and the still-grey sky and the 'smokeless air' did allow me partially at least to enter in to the poet's mood. But the noise of the roadworks on the bridge and from the conversion of County Hall dragged me quickly back to the present.

I came back on to the south side of the river and headed for Waterloo Station. There is only one real way to enter this monumental place and that is through the Victory Arch dedicated to the fallen of World War I. You step through it, and there is tangible proof that their struggle and that of their fallen comrades of the later great conflict did establish a permanent peace in Europe. Because this is the current terminal for the Channel tunnel trains, and such a tunnel would have been unthinkable unless the threat of a European war had been entirely eliminated. The architect got this extension right. It enhances, complements, contrasts its exciting soaring vision with the grandeur of the refurbished original.

Waterloo is the London terminus for passengers from what must be the most affluent suburbs of the city – in Surrey. On the main line to Southampton beyond Clapham Junction and Surbiton lie the restrained Surrey towns of Esher and Walton-on-Thames and Weybridge. Beyond them are Woking and Guildford and Camberley. These are not suburbs served by the London Underground. They are therefore different, more exclusive. In these parts you will find high-flying executives who have already reached their apogee. They work in London, but they are not of London. But they swarm into Waterloo on fast and regular express commuter trains, disgorge onto the multitudinous platforms, and dive into the Waterloo and Bank shuttle – the epitome of exclusive Tube life – which whisks them into the heart of the financial universe. Others, less privileged, catch the Northern or the Bakerloo Lines to less favoured places which exchange their quotas of *hoi polloi* at every stop. If you're not a Waterloo man, don't linger. It will affect your judgment.

I walked through the complex of walkways heading for Waterloo Bridge. Approaching the Royal Festival Hall, I was surprised to come across a bust of Nelson Mandela. The councillors of my own city of Glasgow had offended some people long ago by supporting Mandela's cause, even to the extent of renaming a street 'Nelson Mandela Place'. Naturally, the street chosen was the one where the South African consulate was located, so that the government that had imprisoned him was forced to use his name in their address. And, shortly after his release, Mandela accepted an invitation to visit Glasgow, where he also accepted the freedom of the city. I strode across Waterloo Bridge to the north side again. From here, the view of St Paul's looking just like the Anunciation is a far stronger reminder of Venice than anything at Warwick Avenue. But nobody else seems to notice. Not one person on the bridge looked down the river at the view. The cyclists – green, I'm sure – cycled on, despite the notice prohibiting them.

I continued towards Embankment station and walked up towards Charing Cross. There was something that I wanted to check. Just to the side of Charing Cross station runs Villiers Street. This is the family name of the Dukes of Buckingham, who owned most of the surrounding area. They may still do, for all I know. They certainly stamped their brand on the place. Because the names of the streets spell out George Villiers, Duke of Buckingham, a court favourite of Charles I. I checked them off. There was George Street and Villiers Street. Duke Street was just round the corner, and Buckingham Street was close by. But where was Of Alley? There was no sign of it. After much ferreting around I discovered what had happened. According to the Post Office it has now had its name changed to 'York Place formerly Of Alley'. What spoilsport was responsible for that?

I travelled up the line to Regent's Park. Give an architect like John Nash 500 acres of farmland and a government commission and Regent's Park is what you get. The terraces are simply the best, and surround the park with grandeur.

Refreshed, invigorated, inspired by the Park and its surroundings, I went back down to the rather dilapidated station to complete my journey at Baker Street. As I left my train, I couldn't resist another look at the old station within the station. This, you could say, is where it all began.

CHAPTER EIGHT

LONDON ENCLOSED

The Circle Line is a masterpiece of Underground invention. Like every small boy's toy train set, it runs round and round endlessly, but in both directions. I feel very comfortable going round in circles underground. I've been doing it for years in my native Glasgow. There, the Underground is just a circle, nothing more, but it's full of character. Some of the stations are located where there used to be people, but now there are just motorways. Unlike London, too, there's a well-known song about the Glasgow Underground. I wonder why London's Underground hasn't spawned a popular song?

The Circle Line shares most of its 14-mile route with other lines, and it was co-operation between the two independent companies which ran the District and Metropolitan Lines that led to the possibility, in 1884, of trains travelling in a circle. And this shape makes it unique in London. It serves 27 stations, most of them named after famous London landmarks. It is therefore the ideal tourist line.

But, when you set off on a journey round the Circle Line, where should you start? It's an impossible philosophical question. I suppose it depends where you arrived from. The Circle Line links all the main London railway termini except Waterloo. For my own part, I decided to set off from Tower Hill, because that, near enough, is where the construction of Roman London started.

Here, the station lets you out at the back of the Tower of London. From this perspective, the most ancient and best-known vista, the White Tower, built by William the Conqueror as his home, is obscured. But you get a much better idea of the size of the palace and its wide moat. The moat was drained last century. Today it is grassed. As I passed, the grass was being cut and a marquee erected on it.

Tower Bridge is of much more recent origin. Even close up, it doesn't actually look real. It's too modern and, over-engineered, it looks more like a giant Lego construction than a proper bridge.

Near the station is a large, open, walk-in war memorial to the 24,000 merchant navy and fishing fleet who died in World War II. Reminiscent of the Vietnam Wall in Washington, it contains a garden for contemplation, which people were using to have their lunch. Behind the memorial – and the reason for its location – is Trinity House, from where all England's lighthouses are controlled.

You would not think that, in a city crammed with them, that monument was a sufficiently specific name with which to identify any location, let alone an underground station. But this monument is a memorial of a different kind. It commemorates the Great Fire of 1666. Exactly 202 feet in height, to match the distance it is from the bakery in Pudding Lane where the fire started, the Monument is surrounded by narrow streets and steep hills more reminiscent of Montmartre. It is a reminder of the rabbit warren that was London before the famous three-day conflagration.

Mansion House is, of course, the headquarters of the Lord Mayor of London, and its Underground station was opened on 3 July 1871, linking it directly to Westminster. Despite which, the Lord Mayor of London continued to process to Parliament by means of the Lord Mayor's carriage.

London's Lord Mayor dates back to 1192 in the reign of England's Richard I, who was, as often as not, away on his crusades in the Middle East. In his absence, to counter the influences of the regent (later King) John, municipal rule arose following a French model, with a mayor, supported by a body of aldermen and councillors, in charge. Thus London became the first city to be incorporated. The Corporation of the City of London, as a means of political administration, therefore predates the English Parliament which was not first summoned until 1265. The city had already begun to regard itself as a check on central government and, with hindsight, can be looked upon as an instrument in the spreading of democracy. Thus, when King John was forced to concede the terms of the Magna Carta the Lord Mayor of London was one of the 25 witnesses to the signing and one of two London citizens charged with overseeing its implementation. Robert FitzWalter, castellian of the city, was the other. Among many other things, the Charter recognised the citizens' right to elect their mayor from among themselves, and to present their choice to the sovereign for ratification. The 'ridings' to Westminster to seek the sovereign's approval were the origins of the annual Lord Mayor's Show, which is one of the most popular pageants in London's calendar, beginning and ending at the Mansion House.

With many adjustments to meet the changing circumstances, London had its own local council up until 1986 when central government abolished the Greater London Council. Now, almost unbelievably, the UK's largest city has no local political voice.

The office of Lord Mayor still exists but not as a political figure: mostly, they are drawn from the business world, and elected by members of the Livery Companies of the City of London, who themselves still have to be members of the 25-strong Court of Aldermen.

Temple station is right on the Embankment, land reclaimed from the Thames by Sir Joseph Bazalgatte in 1864. In these days when long-term climatic changes are topics of everyday conversation, mention is often made of the great winters of the past which were so cold that the Thames froze over. Between 1500 and 1814 the river froze solid during 18 winters. Since 1814, it has never frozen completely over, but ice floes and thin ice have appeared during particularly cold spells. Such days will never return, but it's not the fault of global warming. The narrowing of the river as land was reclaimed increased the speed of the flow, so it is unlikely, even if temperatures were to drop dramatically one winter in the future, that the river would ever freeze over again.

Getting off at Temple, I enjoyed the walk in the hot sunshine through the gardens of the Embankment, especially looking at all the statues. It is interesting to see how well the reputation and even the memory of those honoured has or has not survived. You must assume, if someone got a statue here, he (I never saw any women) must have been pretty famous. Yet who now knows anything about Air Marshal Lord Portal, who is described on his pedestal as 'one of the architects of victory in the Second World War'. Oh, really? And that statue was only put up in 1975!

Or what about Sir Henry Bartle Frere (1815–1885), who spent 33 years in India building the ports of Karachi and Bombay and 'did

147

much . . . to help the Indian people'? I'll bet that, however grateful the Indian people were for this help, they managed to restrain themselves from erecting a similar monument to Sir Henry in the city which, the new nationalistic state government has decreed, will henceforth revert to its original name of Mumbai.

Does anyone remember the MP, Sir Wilfred Lawson (1829–1906), who seemed to have wasted the whole of his public life on lost causes? He supported the disestablishment of the Church of England and the abolition of the House of Lords. He defended disarmament and free trade. He also stressed the importance of 'self-discipline and moderation'. A man with whom I would not wish to share a lottery ticket.

But the guy least worth a statue must be Lord Cheylesmore (1848–1925). He was Colonel of the Grenadier Guards, 'although he never saw active service'. Instead, 'he served his country through local government as Mayor of Westminster' . . . and 'as chairman of the National Rifle Association, he *indirectly* (my italics!) did much to improve the marksmanship of the British Army prior to the First World War'. Of all the histories I have read about that bloody conflict, I have never seen accurate shooting listed as a cause of victory. The way the hordes from each side poured over the top, you could hardly miss – or be missed. Anyway, he's there along with some 20 others that I don't recognise.

But there are the ones whom we today would say still deserve their place. Robert Burns for one. Gilbert *and* Sullivan. John Stuart Mill, the philosopher who qualified Benthamism, thus destroying it. Bentham didn't get a statue, but his skeleton was preserved for many years at University College, London. Also worthy of a statue, in relation to the Underground: Isambard Kingdom Brunel, who, in driving the first tunnel under the Thames, allowed the engineers who came after him to develop the Tube.

Cleopatra's Needle is here, too. I think we should give it back to Egypt – the day after the French hand theirs over.

Among the most recent statues is one of a chinthe, the mythical beast which guards Burmese temples and from which Orde Wingate's Chindits took their name. They adopted the motto 'the boldest methods are the safest', which they then proceeded to demonstrate was totally untrue – at least it was for those who died fighting the Japanese.

148

I finished my Embankment walk at Westminster, conscious all the time that not far under my feet rumbled the trains in their pioneering 'cut and cover' culvert – as they had for decades. I felt ready to go underground again. But first, I had to have a look at the Houses of Parliament.

Although the Palace of Westminster is one of the strongest visual images of London, it is really a very recent addition to the capital's treasures. True, on the site there used to be a Saxon palace where Edward the Confessor lived, but nothing remains of that. It was William the Conqueror's son who built the Great Hall which is still in use today. Because of the size of the hall – for decades it was the biggest in Europe – it was the focal point for the ceremonial life of the nation. Increasingly, various types of Councils advising the King met at Westminster. When Henry VIII abandoned it as a royal residence in 1512, it continued to be used by both Houses of Parliament. Its location, outside the city, led to a division between the trade and business centre and the administrative headquarters of London, which is still apparent today.

This mediaeval palace was burned down in 1834 and the building which is there today looks exactly the same as the one which was completed in 1860. Disguised is the fact that German bombs destroyed the chamber of the Commons.

Big Ben, by the way, weighs 13 tons 10 hundredweights and 99 pounds. The minute hand of the great clock is 14 feet long and the minute squares measure a foot. I have always said you can get a real feel for the weight/size/price of an object from the Imperial system measures. Would you prefer 13,650 kilograms, 4.2 metres and 0.3 metres?

I had chosen my day with some forethought. There are so many times of the year when there are interesting happenings at Westminster that I was spoiled for choice. The day I chose to visit Westminster was the day of the announcement of the result of the 1995 Tory leadership campaign. A close result was anticipated, with a second ballot canvassed by the pundits as, at least, an outside possiblity. So all the elements of political drama were present. But the Tory MPs confounded press, pundits and me by tamely re-electing John Major. So the whole day was a bit of damp squib. Redwood, the other leadership candidate, did appear outside the building. He was surrounded by a posse of supporters, Italian-suited and deeply tanned, just like the *mafiosa* they invited comparison with.

But it wasn't just them. All of the MPs, hanging around waiting to be interviewed by about fifty media persons, were strutting around with self-conscious self-importance. I got fed up waiting for something to happen, long before they did, and went off in search of different sensations.

Westminster, of course, is the Tories' naughty council, with all sorts of investigations into corruption and illegalities going on. But they are tough on prostitution. They employ a special cleaning squad to remove prostitutes' calling cards from telephone boxes. These cards, a phenomenon of the Nineties, which add welcome local colour, are to be found in almost all central London phone boxes. Placed there by squads of young men who earn hundreds of pounds a week for the minimal risk that they run, the cards advertise the services and phone numbers of the whole range of call-girls. These are generally described as 'new', 'seventeen' and 'French'. Most of them seem to specialise in 'lessons' and 'discipline'. Anyway, apparently, in three weeks 780,000 cards were removed from 760 booths. The next week, they were all back again.

Also back again, and again, and again, is London's water, recycled apparently several times on its way down the Thames. Water has always been a source of great discussion in London. Pressures of population have ensured that, since the seventeenth century at least, it has always been polluted and the cause of all forms of disease. So, much beer is drunk in England because of fears about the quality of water. I thought all of this had been solved by the dying years of the twentieth century and that the only problem was that, due to total lack of investment in water works, we simply didn't have enough of the stuff – particularly in dry summers like 1995. But not according to Westminster Council. They warn against swimming in the inland waters of their city because 'inland waters are likely to be contaminated with Weil's Disease, which is caused by a virus found in rats' urine. Symptoms are similar to a common cold but, if left untreated, can lead to failure of the liver and kidneys and to rapid death.' How many of the New Year revellers in the Trafalgar Square fountains are taken out by this?

One station on from Westminster, there is almost too much to see from St James's Park . . . the Cabinet War Rooms, Caxton Hall, Buckingham Palace, New Scotland Yard, Westminster Cathedral and St James's Park itself. You don't emerge into the park, or anywhere near it. Rather, you come up to the middle of a busy office district. Above the station itself towers a massive white stone office building.

Turning my back on that, I was surprised to get a full frontal view of Westminster Abbey. I didn't realise that this was the most convenient station for it. Outside the Abbey is a monument to various soldiers. The name most prominently displayed on it was that of Lord Raglan, who was responsible for most of the ghastly mistakes made in that most useless of wars in the Crimea. The clock on Westminster Abbey is on the left tower, whereas that of St Paul's is on the right. I wondered why. Inside, the church is disappointingly small.

St James's Park itself is some way away. I was intrigued by the little house that is perched at the entrance to Duck Island, which isn't an island but a peninsula. This little gem, with its red tiles, wooden bridge and tidy garden, was attracting the tourists, who flock like the ducks to have their pictures taken outside it. There are no cages in Birdcage Walk, but plenty of trees, where birds perched. There didn't seem to be anything exotic.

On the other side of Horse Guards Road, which runs along the park, they are re-building the entrance to the Cabinet War Rooms, such has been its attraction to tourists. Visitors can wander through the 21 rooms – cramped, poorly ventilated and very basic – which Churchill and his staff had to endure for the six long years of the war. Now they are advertised as air-conditioned.

The Palace of St James is the senior palace of the Queen, and is still the Court to which foreign ambassadors are attached. It was built in 1540 by Henry VIII, and a lot of the original brick buildings remain. Henry played tennis – Real Tennis, or Royal tennis, a game resembling squash racquets – here. From here, Prince Henry travelled frequently to the Tower of London to learn navigation from Sir Walter Raleigh, who had been imprisoned by his father, James VI and I.

Now, I don't want to worry those of you who make a habit of using Sloane Square station. But, as you descend into the station, have you ever looked up and noticed a very broad overhead tube? Well, that's not another Tube or a service tunnel. It's the Westbourne River in an enclosed culvert on its way to the Thames, which it joins at Chelsea.

Chelsea, to most people, means the King's Road. But most people don't know that it's called that because it was the King's private road from his palace at Whitehall to his palace at Hampton Court. Romantics who claim that it's because it was the path that Charles II used to walk down to Fulham to meet Nell Gwyn have derived their standards of royal behaviour from introspection. This was the guy whose father had his head cut off. He wasn't going to risk walking about London on his own.

Later, George III did use it, to get to Kew. But he, as we have noted, was mad.

Almost as mad have been the various and ever-changing names given to the stations on the west side of the Circle Line. The Circle, of course, has hardly any tracks of its own – the trains mostly run on the tracks laid down by the early Metropolitan and District railways. Indeed, the Metropolitan cheekily called its horseshoe the 'Inner Circle' long before it linked up with the District Line in 1884.

High Street Kensington was one of a batch of stations opened in October 1868, then known as Kensington (High Street), to distinguish it reasonably enough from Kensington (Addison Road), which was the terminal station on a small and forgotten branch of the Metropolitan Line from Latimer Road, closed in 1940.

Notting Hill Gate, however, also opened in 1868, has never had a name change, though its West Indian population and astonishing annual carnival have changed the face of its streets for ever. Bayswater has been less fortunate, having opened as plain Bayswater, changed to Bayswater (Queen's Road) & Westbourne Grove in 1923, losing its second part in 1933 and unaccountably being renamed Bayswater (Queensway) in 1946 until gradually the suffix was sensibly dropped again.

Paddington had several Underground stations, until they were all linked up. The original 1863 Metropolitan station was in Bishop's Road, while another one was opened at Praed Street on what became the Circle branch in 1868. The Bakerloo Line interleaved itself in 1913, and they all became joined together for better or for worse in

1948. Halfway along the original 1863 line, Portland Road became Great Portland Street in 1917, and acquired Regent's Park in its name for ten years from 1923 before reverting to its present name. While, at the other end of the pioneering journey, the original Farringdon Street station closed after just two years' service in favour of a new one (now called just Farringdon) on the line extending eastwards.

Before Farringdon, however, are the two stations which link into the mainline services to Scotland . . . Euston for the West coast line to Glasgow, which suffered an image body-blow when its much vaunted high speed train, tilting to ride the bends even faster, flopped spectacularly and expensively in the early 1980s. I remember vividly its being sent, with much fuss and fanfare, on its inaugural way from Glasgow Central. It never came back . . . And King's Cross for the East coast line to Edinburgh, which also now carries on to Glasgow, providing a more comfortable and equally fast service by the longer route.

I cannot, of course, think of King's Cross except in terms of the disastrous fire of 18 November 1987, which killed 31 people in scenes of harrowing poignancy. It was started by a match falling through an escalator. Now smoking is banned throughout the entire system.

Above ground, the Barbican looks like a peripheral housing estate. The buildings that are visible from the street are ugly Sixties-type system-built multi-storey monstrosities. But, as the residents are rich, they can make them work. Your typical council house resident is poor and unemployed so the multi-storey is a prison which decays through lack of maintenance. The location is also bad. But the Barbican's location is ideal, with all the entertainments and diversions that Western civilisation can offer at a price on the doorstep.

Ironmongers' Hall is one. With imposing iron gates and stained–glass windows, it sits just off Aldgate Street. Brick on the ground floor, Tudor on the first, it is just what tourists want to see. They should also visit the Museum of London, the only museum that I have accessed by lift. Here, round a sunken garden, past the Dick Whittington and cat motifs and costermonger's barrow, you can get a complete run-down of the history of the city.

To the west of Barbican station is Smithfield Market – the only one of the traditional city centre markets in London which is going to be retained. Covent Garden is a tourist trap; Spitalfields would like to be one, but can't afford it yet; the Caledonian Road cattle market went the way of all antiques before becoming a fairground park; and there are no fish at Billingsgate. But Smithfield, where meat has been traded for a thousand years, has managed to adapt to the demands of modern hygiene and a changing market by spending £70 million on a complete refurbishment. The pubs are open till after breakfast.

Just at the corner of Giltspur Street, high up on the wall, is the Fat Boy or the Golden Boy of Cock Lane. This *mannequin pis* of London is a small monument to the Great Fire of London. It used to have a plaque which suggested that the fire was God's revenge for the gluttony of Londoners, a reference to the fact that the fire started in Pudding Lane and ended near here at Pie Corner.

Heading southwards, I discovered to my surprise on the wall of St Bart's Hospital a plaque commemorating Scotland's greatest patriot, William Wallace. Thought by many to be just another troublemaker, the latest theory is that he was betrayed by another, better–known, Scottish patriot – none other than Robert the Bruce. His henchmen led Wallace to be captured and handed over to the English at Robroyston, just outside Glasgow. At a summary trial for treason at Westminster Hall in August 1305, Wallace protested he could not be accused of treason against a foreign land. But the English tortured and executed him anyway in the most brutal manner, by hanging, drawing and quartering, near to where the memorial now stands. His epitaph reads 'bas agus buaidh'. That means 'death and victory' – at least, so the woman in Glasgow's Gaelic shop told me.

Not far away is a plaque at St John's Gate, the headquarters of one of the orders of chivalry, which was built in 1148 and burned down in 1381 by Wat Tyler – the blacksmith who over 11 days of midsummer madness led England's Peasants' Revolt – 300 years before the French revolution and 500 years before the October revolution in Russia. The original Essex man (he was from Kent, but why spoil a good phrase?), Tyler's mistake, like today's Essex men, was not knowing when to stop demanding more. By marching on London at the head of an army of 10,000 peasants, he had already wrung as many concessions for peasants as he was likely to secure. Incredibly, the king had agreed the abolition of serfdom and all feudal services, the removal of restrictions on freedom of labour and trade, the enfranchisement of villeins and the institution of social equality. But, even as he shook hands with the 14-year-old Richard II, who had just agreed to his latest demands, he couldn't resist insulting him. One of the king's most chivalrous knights, the Mayor of London, Sir William Walworth, ran him through with his sword. Tyler was taken to St Bart's – not a privilege offered to many peasants – but there he died a peasant's death. Walworth Road is, of course, where the Labour Party now has its London headquarters.

Incidentally, the spark that lit the Peasants' Revolt was, yes, you've guessed it, the imposition of a poll tax! Some 850 years later Margaret Thatcher tried the same trick. History repeated itself when the peasants revolted again.

Finding the Barbican Arts Centre is easier than anyone who visited it ever admitted. It is not the maze of legend. All you do is follow the extremely clear signs and you get there – first time, no problem. After your concert/meeting/conference, you can have the confidence to walk around the housing and stumble across some real oddities – like a bit (just a bit) of the tree under which Mendelssohn (1809–47) composed maybe his 'Fingal's Cave' overture or something equally unlikely after he returned from Scotland. This beech was 500 years old when it fell down in Burnham Woods, in Buckinghamshire. I wonder what happened to the rest of it. Maybe it moved to Dunsinane.

Outside Bow Church, whose bells are midwives to all true cockneys, is a plaque to John Milton, who worshipped there.

With antique pillars massy proof,
And storied windows richly delight,
Casting a dim religious light.
There let the pealing organ blow,
To the full-voiced quire below,
In service high, and anthems clear
As may, with sweetness, through mine ear,
Dissolve me into ecstasies,
And bring Heaven before mine eyes.

Il Penseroso

155

And, in a little square of grass, there is a statue of Captain John Smith, 'Citizen and Cordwainer, 1580–1631, First among the leaders of the settlement at Jamestown from which began the overseas expansion of the English-speaking people'. Which doesn't tell you the most interesting thing about him. He was the man Pocahontas saved.

It happened like this. He was one of the emigrants to the first British settlement in America, Jamestown in Virginia. There you can still see the foundations and broken walls of their little houses in the swamp and marvel at their bravery. He wandered off into the forest one day and was captured by natives. They were about to do a William Wallace on him when Pocahontas, the chief's daughter, threw herself on his neck and pleaded for his life. She later married another Englishman and would have lived happily ever after, except that he took her back to London where she died of smallpox. She is buried in Gravesend but, as that is not on the Underground system, I don't know whether her epitaph acknowledges that from her flowed the overseas expansion of American tourism, or a very successful Disney movie.

At Barbican, you have a choice of Metropolitan, Circle or Hammersmith and City Lines. A fun thing to do is to stand on the enclosed bridge and watch the choice of trains, picking the first suitable one. Like me, you will then miss it because of congestion on the stairs down.

I caught the next one, past Moorgate to Liverpool Street. Liverpool Street station has been extensively modernised. Above ground, British Rail have done a terrific job. It looks so good, with its glass and white tubular piping, that I saw it as London's answer to the Gare de Quai d'Orsay in Paris. But, while that is now the Impressionist museum, Liverpool Street is a live, working station.

Outside, the new architecture matches the challenge set by the station. The building at 100 Liverpool Street is covered in great hanging plants which blend with the red and black finish of its interior. It houses the SGB bank. But the Great Eastern Hotel has not fared so well. Tired and ill, it was advertising a sale of cheap golf clubs the day I was there. But everything about the look of the place would put you off buying a drink, never mind a set of clubs. So I descended again into the Tube, to complete my circular journey at Tower Hill. Forward to the past.

CHAPTER NINE

TUPPENCE COLOURED

There's something attractively direct about the Central Line. No nonsense, no fuss, it just drives its tunnels straight through the middle of London, east to west, west to east. Only in its extremities does it mess about with branches. So every train rumbles under such redolent places as St Paul's, Tottenham Court Road, Oxford Circus, Bond Street and Marble Arch.

The original section of the Central Line was inaugurated by the Prince of Wales in 1900. Its construction reversed a recommendation of the Royal Commission of 1846 that no railway should penetrate the inner London area between the Thames and the New Road (the road which is now Marylebone, Euston and Pentonville Roads).

Parliament had refused a number of proposals for a railway to take advantage of the high volume traffic in this area. But the sanctioning of the Central Line recognised the new reality, and on 30 July 1900, the new east–west cross-London route between Bank and Shepherd's Bush opened with a flat fare of twopence. The 'Tuppenny Tube', as it was inevitably dubbed by the popular press, was very well patronised right from the start – much to the embarrassment of the politicians who had opposed it for so long. They recovered quickly enough, however, to claim credit for the benefits that it brought. Today, the Central Line is the Underground's third busiest line, with 142 million passenger journeys a year.

Popular myth has it that Oxford Circus is the very centre of London, and you might therefore think that this would also be the busiest station. Not so. Its 73 million passenger movements in a typical year are second to Victoria's 80 million. But it is still a lot of people. To accommodate them, in the 1970s, London Transport literally raised the roof over Oxford Circus to build a new central concourse and ticket office. To make this possible, the traffic above had to negotiate an artificial hill and drive over a temporary 'umbrella' of steel which was erected to allow work to proceed relatively undisturbed underneath. Now, Oxford Circus has the true feel of a hub station. Its 14 escalators – more than any other station on the network, carry passengers down to three different pairs of platforms, serving not only the Central Line but also the Victoria and Bakerloo Lines. It is always very busy.

I have no doubt that most visitors to the city would find themselves at Oxford Circus at some stage or other, because that's where London's window shopping is at its best. I wandered round the area in a series of star-shaped walks – up the north side of Oxford Street going eastwards . . . back to Oxford Circus on the south side . . . southwards along the east side of Regent Street past Hamleys, the world's most famous toy shop, and the mock-Tudor frontage of Liberty's fashion store down to Piccadilly Circus . . . back to Oxford Circus on the other side of the road past numerous airline offices and travel agencies . . . westwards along the south side of Oxford Street, taking in the jewellers' paradise of Bond Street as a small diversion . . . then back to the centre along the north side of Oxford Street, where the shops seem somehow slightly downmarket in comparative terms.

Nowhere else in the world in such a small space is it possible to take in so many superior stores. It is easy to spend an entire day in this area, just looking longingly at the inventive and creative window displays. I would imagine a winner of the National Lottery jackpot would find no difficulty in spending the lot of his winnings here within a similar period. I looked at, and longed for, and bought an ice-cream cone for £1.50. Like the other retailers in the area, the ice-cream salesman was operating in a seller's market. It was 90 degrees in the shade.

My northerly walk from Oxford Circus took me to the BBC headquarters – that inspirational, purpose-built building contoured to the shape of the streets at the junction of Portland Place. It has this curious bow-shaped frontage, with a heroic bowsprit sculpture of a human family by none other than Eric Gill, designer of the typeface. The whole effect reminds you of a ship-of-the-line sailing stoically on through rough seas and smooth, but always unperturbed. That indeed was how it was during the dark years of World War II, when this building somehow largely survived the bombing while those within it stuck to their vital tasks.

The Central Line provides the longest possible journey without a change, from Epping to West Ruislip, which is just over 34 miles. It also combines one of the most heavily-used sections, Liverpool Street to Stratford, with one of the least used, at the Epping end.

The reason that a suburban rapid transit system ever extended so far out into rural England is in the best traditions of bungling British bureaucracy. This part of the line was built by the Great Eastern Railway in 1865. It was scheduled for closure before World War II, but then Ongar came into the reckoning as a new town and the railway instead became part of the plan to electrify the Central Line. This modernisation was postponed for the duration of the war. It was revived afterwards, but the electrification was only authorised as far as Loughton. By mistake, London Transport completed the task up to Epping. Indeed, beyond Epping used to be a six-mile, three-station extension to Ongar, which was served by a three-car shuttle train – until it was closed in 1994 for lack of use.

Ongar, which never did become a new town, is archetypically and anonymously Essex and used to be the most northerly point on the Underground network, 24 miles from Oxford Circus. This must be the only occasion in modern times when the London Underground system has actually shrunk – the old threat, 'use it or lose it', actually came to pass.

Nowadays, the Central Line also takes in that curious Underground by-pass, the Waterloo and City Line. This 2,500-yard tube shuttle speeds members of the élite financial services sector from their Surrey main railway terminus to the heart of Bank of England country. It was opened in 1898, but until 1994 was separately managed by British Rail and its predecessors.

Using Oxford Circus as my starting point, I decided to explore the Central Line first in an easterly direction. I stayed on the train through Holborn. I always associate Holborn with Gamages, the famous store from where, in the Fifties, I used to be sent wonderful magic tricks from their mail-order catalogue. Thanks to them, I am today an accomplished conjuror and juggler. At least, so my mother tells me. Holborn was also the scene of the 1960s BBC television sci-fi thriller *Quatermass and the Pit*, which I refused to watch even from behind the couch around which my sister peeped out at the flickering, grey screen.

But the railway Tube has mysteries of its own. In particular, ghost stories abound. Take this very station, Holborn. On 29 November 1955, *The Star* reported 'West Indian porter' Victor Locker (19) as saying, 'I saw the man with his arms outstretched towards me in the staff mess-room at Covent Garden'. Foreman ticket-collector Jack Hayden added, 'I was in the mess-room a week ago and, through the door, I saw the figure of a tall, thin, grey-suited man wearing gloves. I went out to him – but he had gone. I think he was a passenger.' An enquiry was mounted into the 'Tube Line Ghost'. But there is nothing in the story which gives any clue as to why the man was thought to be a ghost in the first place. I don't suppose there is any evidence to support the ticket-collector's contention that he was a passenger. It reminds me of the old joke about the dissatisfied customer complaining about the chef. The angry chef storms out of the kitchen demanding to know who called the chef an idiot. 'Who called the idiot a chef?' came the shout back from the disgruntled diner.

Between Holborn and Chancery Lane (where you'll find the shortest escalator on the network – 50 steps rising just 15 feet) is another well-guarded pillar of the British establishment – the judicial system. But before I began on that, I diverted off Chancery Lane into the London Silver Vaults.

Having just seen the name on the map, I didn't know what kind of security clearance I would need. I envisaged silver bars stacked up behind iron bars. But I got through the door unchallenged and down the stairs to the vaults. Outside were display cabinets showing the most intricate of silverwork, although the silver-gilt icon of the Madonna of Kazan looked like a framed family portrait, which maybe was exactly the effect intended. More likely that the designers of cheap photo frames had been here before me.

I passed through hugely deep doors, deeper than from my finger to elbow (the biblical cubit) into the vaults themselves. What a disappointment. These weren't vaults. They were jewellers' shops, 74 of them. And, this early in the morning, you could hear them counting the spoons. John Tann seemed to play a fairly significant role, the M and S of silversmiths, if the number of shops he had was anything to go by.

Many of the shops had a big piece of display jewellery to attract buyers inside. The most intriguing was the Royal Hunt Cup designed by C.B. Birch for competition at Ascot in 1892. It was won by Lord Rosslyn's Suspender, a bay colt by Muncaster out of Garterless, which won at 25 to 1. You learn something new every day. I wouldn't have believed that suspenders had been invented in 1892.

The alarm went off as I wandered around among the American tourists, none of whom looked as if they had the slightest intention of buying anything. But, just as people do when a car alarm sounds in the street or when a house alarm goes off in the middle of the day, the urgent bell was ignored. And eventually it went away.

I walked down Chancery Lane, turning right on to the Strand, the name another reminder of the tidal Thames. Sitting right in the middle of the road is an ugly big monument with a dragon on top. The inscription is awkwardly placed, too, running all the way round the square structure. With the flow of traffic it was hazardous to try and read it. But, defying the odds on your behalf, I managed to decipher the message. It was erected to indicate the original site of the Temple Bar. Not worth knowing, really.

For anyone wanting to study how the British establishment conserves the best for itself, a visit to at least one of the four Inns of Court, where barristers are trained and practise, is obligatory. The entrance to the Inner Temple is unprepossessing, guarding a secret. Look for Prince Henry's Room and walk through the passageway underneath it. Originally this room was part of the Prince's Inn which escaped the Great Fire of 1666. It is called after the elder son of James VI (of Scotland, that is, but you know that by now) or James I, if you must. Henry was Prince of Wales, but he never made the top job, dying in 1612, thirteen years before his father. This was James's second son's lucky day. Or so the future Charles I may have thought! Would Henry have been more adroit at saving his neck than his brother? And, if so, would constitutional monarchy have come sooner or later if he had become King? There is a television series waiting to be made out of such questions. I would have visited the Room itself, but it was shut for renovation. They left it rather a long time.

161

I walked through the archway into the gaslit Inner Temple, past the twelfth-century Temple Church, one of the five round churches left in England. Originally the headquarters of the Order of Knights Templar, it has belonged for several centuries to the Inns of Court.

Just a few yards from the busy Strand and Fleet Street, the ambience in here is tranquil, studious and reserved. There are paved courtyards and cultured lawns, surrounded by earnest offices and demure flats. The whole place oozes of the class and aloofness of a campus of one of the older universities. The size of the Master's house alone is an indication of the long pedigree of the earnings of barristers.

Back across the Strand stand the Royal Courts of Justice, a nineteenth century neo-Gothic building, representing the permanence, dignity and neutrality of the law, at least presenting that façade, and maybe only that, if some recent cases are the judge.

Wandering back along the Strand, at the edge of Fleet Street, is a memorial to Lord Northcliffe, in his day the most feared of the Fleet Street barons, on the wall of St Dunstan's-in-the-West. Alfred Charles William Harmsworth, Viscount Northcliffe, had an interesting family. He was born in Dublin in 1865; his father was a barrister-at-law of the Middle Temple, having descended from an old Hampshire family. Fred was the eldest of 14 offspring, including seven sons. The next male sibling became Lord Rothermere; the next, a Liberal MP, held government office as under-secretary for home affairs and foreign affairs; the fourth, Robert Leicester, was Liberal MP for Caithness for 22 years. The third youngest son was editor of the *New Liberal Review*, and the youngest seemed not to have made his mark at all. But I reckon it was the second youngest of the Harmsworth boys, St John by name, who really knew how to sustain the family fortune. He is credited with the creation of the Perrier mineral water business! And you (and I) thought it was French. Eau dear!

A far more impressive memorial to the power of the press is inlaid in ornate mosaic on the adjacent gable end. It reads, simply, 'Dundee Courier, People's Journal, People's Friend, Sunday Post'. These are the premises of D.C.Thomson, the world-famous Dundee-based group which produced immortal characters like Dennis the Menace and Desperate Dan and – less importantly – trained half the world's journalists, including people like the legendary James Cameron. These are now the last newspaper offices left in Fleet Street, the rest having scarpered to Canary Wharf and other out-of-town industrial estates.

Back on the Central Line train, I hurried to St Paul's. The station has a nice antique sign at the bottom of the escalator, ushering you 'To The Street'. The exit from the station introduces you to a back view of the cathedral. In fact, you can only just see the dome peeking above the surrounding office blocks. But this is an ideal way in, because it forces you to walk the whole length of the side of the building, making you appreciate how long it is. Unlike most city centre churches, it has a proper churchyard with tall, mature trees. They should be mature, because Wren began building it in 1675. But, of course, it was extensively damaged during World War II. I don't know how the trees survived.

In a little enclosure off to the side, I gained some idea of the scale of the building by a statue that had been taken down for repair. I also formed some impression of the effect of centuries of pollution from the amount of erosion of the face.

Onwards I travelled into *EastEnders* land, Bethnal Green and Mile End, where people who are the 'salt of the earth' survived the Blitz . . . where every corner has a community pub, and the cosmopolitan melting pot that is London is supposedly encapsulated. I discovered, too, that long before its present image was established, Bethnal Green was a well-known silk-weaving area and a centre for the leather trade. It also has its own Roman Road, so it presumably goes back two millennia. But it was always characterised as being a 'poor' district.

The Central Line eastwards emerges briefly into daylight just before drawing up at the art-deco tiled station at Stratford, a quite awful place on the edge of the Essex marshes which, so far as I can tell, owes nothing to the art-deco movement. This is not, of course, Stratford-upon-Avon, and the nearest Shakespearean connection is most probably the new Globe Theatre on the south side of the Thames, best accessed from London Bridge on the Northern Line. This Stratford, however, is mentioned in the *Canterbury Tales* so, thanks to Chaucer, it does have its own literary connections.

From Stratford, the train then dives steeply into darkness again before emerging into daylight for the rest of the journey towards Epping at Leyton. Here, there is a small cemetery which abuts the line. Like so many in public hands, it is overgrown and rather neglected, and I saw only one couple walking in summer clothes between the low headstones. The largest memorial was tucked over to one side and was to the war dead.

This bit of the Underground was constructed immediately before World War II, and was nearly completed then. But the intervention of the war postponed its opening. Indeed, the tunnels at Redbridge, for example, were used by Plessey for the manufacture of aircraft parts. Extensive use was made of concrete as an architectural design material for the surface buildings. Unfortunately, pre-war concrete technology was insufficiently understood, and the corrosive effect of the British weather has taken its toll over the past 60 years.

A ticket check at Leytonstone found me in possession of a valid ticket, thus depriving me of the opportunity of discovering whether or not the inspector had been recruited from the ranks of master butchers or consultant cardiologists. At Leytonstone, you can take the alternative branch which loops rectangularly to Hainault 'via Newbury Park', as the destination boards always tell you. Nothing happens at Newbury Park: it is simple Essex suburbia. On the way there, though, the line dives again into a tube which runs directly beneath the great Eastern Avenue thoroughfare, which must have been one of the first post-war dual carriageways, lined with terraced yellow-brick housing and one of the earliest dedicated cycle paths.

A shallow 40 feet or so under, the Central Line carries its passengers rapidly through Redbridge, Gants Hill (above ground, it used to be just a big roundabout, now, it's a magnificently rebuilt modern palazzio, looking remarkably like one of Moscow's grander stations), Newbury Park, Barkingside and Fairlop to Hainault. The train that I occupied was the emptiest I had experienced in all of my journeys. So I wondered what all those people in cars up above were thinking of, when they had such convenience (and cleanliness) beneath the streets.

At Hainault, where there's a major train maintenance depot, you used to walk across to another train which shuttled you to Woodford and back past three more stations. Now, though, every second train goes all the way round the loop.

I just had to get off at Grange Hill to look for the school where Susan Ross was educated before she left to become an *EastEnder* and to have her baby as Michelle Fowler. Although Hainault High School is indicated on the local map thoughtfully provided at many of these outlying stations, when I reached it I was disappointed. It didn't coincide with my memory of the real Grange Hill. But was it, I wondered, the prototype? I rang Phil Edmond, who created the programme. 'No,' he said. 'The series was originally called Grange Park, but there were so many real schools of that name that we changed it to Grange Hill. Three years after the series started I was sitting on the Tube and was amazed to find myself in Grange Hill station. That was the first I knew that it existed.'

At Woodford, where Sir Winston Churchill was the Member of Parliament when he was Prime Minister, you can rejoin the main service to Epping. Onwards to Loughton, where there was a hilltop camp during the Iron Age and the Romans drove their road from London to Chigwell (which they dubbed Little London) a few years before the Great Eastern Railway. At the town's grammar school, William Penn, the Quaker who founded Pennsylvania, received part of his education.

Next along the line, Buckhurst Hill, 'the hill of the beech trees', which I discovered was part of a huge hunting area which entertained Henry VIII and Anne Boleyn. Whereas it was Loughton that was favoured by James VI. The eastern landscape of the London Underground system felt much less familiar than the north or west. The topography is subtly different, the land lower-lying, with a less fertile look about it. However, after Buckhurst Hill, the appearance of cows signalled the start of the green belt. A sign indicated a 'permissive footpath' through the fields. Whatever that is and wherever it led, I would like to have walked it. But the train rushed on.

Theydon Bois – Theydon, the thatched valley, whatever that means, and Bois, the family name of the lords of the manor in the twelfth century (a case of not seeing the wood for the forest?) – is now a pleasant little community that places great stress on the 20 or so voluntary organisations which help residents pass many a cold winter evening. It boasts the only herd of wild, black, fallow deer in the UK. The relaxed, rural feel was emphasised by the window cleaner, ladder over his shoulder, walking casually from one bungalow to another in a neat little estate on the outskirts of Epping – which I discovered means upland in Anglo-Saxon.

Here I was on the edge of the great forest which used to cover the whole of West Essex. Now only a tenth of its size, it still stretches into the outer fringes of London. It was once the most famous of Royal hunting forests. When that use declined, it was enclosed and encroached upon. Its survival is thanks to the unlikely intervention of the Corporation of the City of London who, through their ownership of about 200 acres, put pressure on the other lords of the manors and eventually, in 1878, ended up acquiring all their rights and becoming Conservators of the Forest in lieu of the crown. It was here that Boadicea made her last stand against the Romans. And here Dick Turpin shot a forester in 1737. The wanted poster described him as of only average height with a smallpox-marked face. It never mentioned the horse.

Epping today hides its violent past well. The station itself has a small garden attached to it, where a variety of flowers and vegetables were being grown. There were peas and potatoes – and even a grapevine hidden among the ivy which climbed the brick wall. A home-made garden bench confirmed the impression that time moves slower here. The guard chatted languidly to the driver in the warm sunshine. It was not the kind of thing you would see in the pressure cauldron of Piccadilly Circus. Indeed, out here or at the end of any line, it is easy to forget that you are on part of the same system that took you through the frenetic activity of central London, with all its pushing and shoving and overcrowding and perspiration.

From the bridge just beyond the station you can look on to the rusting line to Ongar, draped with orange netting to indicate its closure. It's said that this line was so little used latterly that, when the ancient rolling stock broke down, London Transport just put the passengers into taxis – and saved money! Its closure meant that I could not now visit Blake Hill station which once held the world record for the lowest number of passengers, 32 per week.

A more creditable claim to fame is that it was here that John Betjeman worked as a station-master to experience the life, the better to write about it. George Orwell worked as a 'plongeur' in the restaurants of Paris for much the same reason. But Betjeman was no more locked into the monotony and restrictiveness of life on the railway than Orwell was destitute. When he wrote the book he was a graduate waiting to take up a teaching post back in England, not a down-and-out without a future.

But, as the price of government agreement to the closure, the Epping–Ongar section had to be offered for sale to any interested private operating company. An advertisement duly appeared in the *Financial Times* in June 1995, the prospects held out that the line might one day revert to steam, under the auspices of the Ongar Railway Preservation Society which wants to establish a steam leisure centre in the town.

Epping does leave you wanting more. Who could resist names like Chipping Ongar, or Lower Nazeing or Bumbles Green? Perhaps one day, an extended London Underground will introduce them to me.

From Oxford Circus, the westbound trains hurtle at apparently breakneck speed – actually a maximum of 60mph and an average of 20.5mph – past the diplomatic quarter of Marble Arch and Lancaster Gate. Marble Arch is out of place. It was originally erected in front of Buckingham Palace to represent the Spirit of England. But it was moved in 1851 to its present position, which used to be the site of Tyburn Gallows. Surrounded as it is by roads and traffic, it's not really worth a special visit.

There are two Underground stations from which you can approach Kensington Palace – High Street Kensington or Queensway. I preferred the Queensway route from the Central Line. This allowed me to wander down the Broad Walk through Kensington Palace Gardens, with the Round Pool on my left, until I came to the Palace itself.

It was Queen Victoria who moved the official Royal London residence from here to the much newer Buckingham Palace. Strange, because not only was she born at Kensington but there, too, she heard of her accession on the death at the age of 72 of her uncle, William IV, who had reigned for only seven years. He was the last monarch to attempt to impose an unpopular government on the British Parliament, although Queen Victoria tried her best to promote her favourite, Disraeli, irrespective of the arithmetic of the elections.

Kensington Palace was a Jacobean House which Wren was asked to renovate so that William and Mary could move from a Whitehall which they considered to be cold and damp. For someone from Scotland visiting London in the middle of summer this complaint was about as valid as one the lady in the song makes about California. Not that Mary was a tramp . . .

Princess Margaret has had a 20-room apartment here for years. Newer 'tenants' include Prince and Princess Michael of Kent, the Duke and Duchess of Gloucester and the Princess of Wales. Kensington Palace also houses in the State Apartments a collection of court dresses from 1750 to 1940. But it's the Palace's role as a Royal council block that intrigues me. Do they pop in and out for a chat and to borrow cups of sugar? A soap based here would run longer than *Neighbours*. They could call it *Eldorado*.

More interesting, too, is the rectangular Palace Garden surrounded by a thick hedge of sycamore, I guess (but I'm no arborologist), with holes cut in each of its sides, allowing you to look in on three fountains playing on the lily pond. The garden is formally laid out, and the flowers and shrubs are all carefully selected in pastel colours. A fat thrush bounced for worms and an even fatter pigeon sat sunning itself. The gardeners have created a wonderful feeling of restfulness in the middle of the busy city. For the first time I realised the art that there could be in gardening, because there was more than a collection of plants here. An atmosphere had been captured. Far more impressive in its creativity than Kew. But I had to leave. The Palace was shutting early for a private Royal party. The footpersons did it in a friendly and polite way.

Most people equate Shepherd's Bush (where there are two quite separate Underground stations about 200 yards apart, which do not connect with each other except by exiting to the street) with the BBC Television studios. The BBC did occupy an old film studio complex at Lime Grove for many years after the war. Programmes such as *Tonight* and Richard Dimbleby's *Panorama* emanated from Lime Grove, which was a hop and a skip from the Hammersmith & City Line high-level station at Shepherd's Bush, or a ten-minute walk to the new Television Centre at White City. But the Lime Grove studios were finally abandoned by the BBC in 1990, and are now demolished. The BBC also abandoned the Shepherd's Bush Theatre, which it had used for the production of a huge variety of popular and well-known entertainment programmes in front of invited audiences – from Val Doonican's shows to *TW3*.

Shepherd's Bush was the western terminus of the original Central Line opened in 1900. Now, it is just another station and, above ground, Shepherd's Bush is just a huge traffic roundabout, notable only for its traditional street market – and even that lacks the atmosphere it once had.

At White City station, you can sit on old-fashioned wooden benches surmounted by what appeared to be some of the original old Underground logo signs made of cast iron. Like most of the Underground's station furniture, they have a touch of craftsmanship about them. And they appear to have more of the craftman's personal touch than today's technologically designed and produced equipment can possibly have. I wondered what happened to all the rest of them. Were they melted down to pig iron and recycled into refrigerator panels? Or are they lying forgotten and forlorn in some London Transport depot, awaiting their sudden discovery as an item of unexpected value in the BBC's *Antiques Roadshow*? The answer, I discovered, is more prosaic: they were sold off by London Transport as memorabilia, for £150,000.

The *Antiques Roadshow* is not produced by the BBC from its impressive Television Centre at White City. Antiques come from Bristol! In fact, so much of the BBC's output these days is produced from 'the regions' that the Television Centre is in danger of being pensioned off. It was originally conceived on the back of the ubiquitous envelope by Graham Dawbarn of architects Norman Dawbarn in 1949. He was confronted with a roughly triangular site to the south of the White City stadium, which had lain little-used since it had been the location for the 1908 Olympic Games and the odd exhibition. Given the constraints of the site and the peculiar requirements of the BBC, he came up with a unique building in the shape of a question mark – a highly appropriate symbol of our national broadcaster.

The main part of the building was to be effectively circular, with six or seven studios radiating out from behind the offices which looked out on to the central courtyard. An outer ring road provided access for servicing vehicles bringing in scenery and supplies. Future extensions were envisaged in the form of the 'tail' of the question mark, heading northwards towards White City stadium.

When you go to the BBC Television Centre now, you are immediately astonished at how accurately the finished building reflects the original concept. And how modern the place still seems, even though the first part of it was finished and in use by 1957. Nearly 40 years later, it seems as fresh and sprightly as it must have when new, even though the technology inside has changed out of all recognition.

Nowadays, though, it is not the fun palace it once was. The place is dominated by the News and Current Affairs department, which from its HQ in the 'tail' spreads its all-enveloping tentacles throughout the circular corridors, overwhelming the creations of other departments and commandeering their airspace at the merest whiff of yet another political mini-sensation. The tail certainly wags the dog at the BBC Television Centre. It is, nevertheless, a fascinating place, and a tour of the BBC studios is one of the best days out that any organisation could arrange.

Beyond Shepherd's Bush and White City on the Central Line lies Acton, which boasts not one but four stations. To get to West Acton, you have to take the two-station branch to Ealing Broadway. But I'd already been there, on the District Line train which happens also to pass through Acton Town.

On the Central Line, East Acton is a little wooden station with a bizarre and anachronistic rural feel about it. The unexpectedly neat red brick houses are a model of social responsibility. Everywhere there are signs of law-abidingness. There are 'No ball games' notices on walls and on open spaces. And, unexpectedly, there were no ball games being played. There were 'No cycling' signs. And, astonishingly, there was no cycling. There was even a prohibition notice erected by the GLC which had survived that council's demise. And there were traffic-calming measures which slowed everything down.

The only sinister note was struck by Henchman Street. But, of course, I was looking for signs because I knew that I was just around the corner from Wormwood Scrubs. Work began there to build a prison to hold 1,000 prisoners in 1874 and it took an incredibly long 16 years to complete. On the towers which flank the main gate are two profiles like huge cameo brooches. They depict two great prison reformers, Elizabeth Fry and John Howard. The prison was used by MI5 during the war. George Blake escaped from here, or was let out by the same intelligence service. It now houses under 700 prisoners in categories A, B, C, and D. What I took to be staff quarters were semi-inhabited and semi-derelict. If that is where they house the warders, I thought, what do the prisoners get?

But appearances are misleading, as to the long-term prospects, at least. There has been a major refurbishment in progress for the past few years to install toilets in cells, a 90-bed hospital, kitchen, reception, gymnasium, education facilities, workshops and additional cell space. According to Governor Jackson, the refurbishment will give the prison the longest ridge roof in London. According to me, this will allow the prisoners of the twenty-first century ample space and plenty of roof tiles for effective high-level protest.

I hurried on past North Acton and Hanger Lane into the heart of Middlesex. To Northolt, from where the RAF played a vital role in the Battle of Britain. It was the home of III Fighter Squadron, which was the first to fly Hurricanes. In September 1940 alone, 100 German aeroplanes were shot down by 'planes based at Northolt. It was also the base for the Free Polish Air Force.

At Greenford, they boast of a unique Underground curiosity: the escalators don't go down to the trains, they go up! Otherwise, the place is no longer green or its houses affordable, even in these days of negative equity.

Ruislip is another place with four stations on the Underground system. Five, if you count Ruislip Manor which, like Ruislip itself, is on the Metropolitan Line. On the Central Line, you pass through South Ruislip and Ruislip Gardens to get to West Ruislip, the terminus.

A major modernisation scheme for the Central Line has just been completed, at a cost of £840 million. From the public's point of view, the chief benefit is the fleet of ultra-modern carriages. How long, I wonder, will they remain so good-looking and comfortable. It's a sad commentary that two of the 'bullet points' about the new features of these trains is their 'vandal-resistant paint' and the 'security-conscious larger windows in the ends of cars'.

But the 85 new trains are certainly smoother and brighter, with good in-car communications. There is also a new automatic computer-based train control and signalling system which is an enhanced version of what has been 'well tested and proven in Singapore and Hong Kong'. Once, it was the other way round in these far-flung corners of the Commonwealth! But now even Spain is ahead of us with the system also up and running in Madrid.

At the depot just after Ruislip Gardens, there is also an impressive new train wash facility. Like a car wash, only longer, it's just part of the unseen and taken-for-granted infrastructure of services and servicing which the everyday Underground passenger never thinks about.

It was about the same time that I discovered that the Central Line trains are air-conditioned – or at least a draught blows up from vents behind the seats. Out here it was certainly pleasant, but it didn't really cope with the heat of town. And, having no fans, the system depends on the movement of the train. Not much good if you are stuck in a tunnel.

From just across the road at the West Ruislip terminus, you can see the countryside poking up in the distance, beckoning you to stay, or venture further into the Chiltern confluence of Berkshire, Buckinghamshire and Hertfordshire. Dick Whittington-like, I turned again.

CHAPTER TEN

VICTORIAN VALUES

The bald statistics of the Underground are impressive. If you multiply all the people who use the Tube by all the journeys that they made, you can figure out how busy the Tube is. So, if I travel to work and back on the one tube line every day, five days a week for a year (2x5x52), then that's 520 passenger journeys. The total for the Underground in 1995 was 764 million passenger journeys. The distance that all of the passengers put together travelled on all of their journeys was 6,051 million kilometres.

If you add up all the journeys made by all of the trains put together, then you get 55 million kilometres, but that's less than half way to the sun.

I would love to give you all of those distances in good old miles, which would give both of us a better chance of grasping them. But I can't. Because, sadly, note 1 on page 23 of the accounts of London Underground Ltd for the year ended 31 March 1995 states that 'the Unit of Measurement Directive, adopted by the European Community, requires bodies such as London Underground Limited to use the metric system of measurement in their publications and to have ceased using the Imperial system of measurement by 1 January 1995. The figures for previous years have been restated accordingly.' Napoleon rules, OK?

That year the Underground charged an average fare of 10.3 pence per passenger kilometre – compare that to the 30-odd pence that a salesman or woman would claim back from the company in car expenses. The average waiting time was 3 minutes 12 seconds, which the average passenger would have to concede is pretty good – and certainly a lot better than the average waiting time for the bus of your choice (nothing for half an hour, then three in a bunch!).

In 1995, the London Underground had a turnover of £765 million.

Compare that to British Airways, which is ten times bigger, or to Marks and Spencer with a turnover of £6.8 billion. Some people might be surprised by this, but the Underground made an accounting loss of £307 million, which was covered by government grant. It did, however, employ over 17,000 people, including 479 police officers. And it had assets of six and a half billion pounds.

I was playing with all of these calculations, as I waited to begin my next journey from Brixton at one end of the Victoria Line to Walthamstow at the other. The Victoria Line was the first London Tube line to be built since the early twentieth-century expansion which followed the development of electric traction. Planned originally in 1943, and completed in stages between 1968 and 1971, the Victoria is the only one which is entirely underground. It penetrates areas of the city which had until then somehow, remarkably, remained 'Tubeless'. It links four British Rail terminal stations, and passes through the three busiest stations, Victoria, Oxford Circus and King's Cross. The Victoria was also London's first 'automatic' tube. Once the doors are closed and the driver's twin start buttons are pressed, the trains operate automatically, controlled by coded impulses transmitted through the track.

This line saw the first of the new generation aluminium-bodied carriages, bright, light, clean and airy. They made the rickety old rolling stock of the Glasgow Underground look positively antediluvian – which of course they were, because they were the original carriages of 1896. The Glasgow Underground had developed some very folksy characteristics – such as the famous 'shoogle' which shook passengers from side to side throughout the journey, and the infamous smell, which is almost indescribable, but was a strange mixture of cookery and drains – kind of sweet and sour.

Inspired by the new London Tube trains, Glasgow's Underground was completely refurbished in the 1970s to remove both the shoogle and the smell, which it successfully did – much to the chagrin of the traditionalists!

Now the Victoria Line trains have been refurbished and repainted in anti-graffiti paint. The mind boggles that graffiti paint sprayers are still able to do their ridiculous damage to trains which spend their entire lives underground! Or possibly it's because the trains were liable to be vandalised on their way back from refurbishment. This took place not at some depot in London, but 400 miles away at the former Royal Naval Dockyard at Rosyth, on the northern shores of the Firth of Forth in Scotland, beside the Forth bridges!

There was little along the line that caught my fancy that was not better covered by another line. So, I decided to travel on the Victoria Line from one end to the other, with as few stops as possible at the 16 stations in between, from Brixton in the south to Walthamstow in the north. Without interruptions, the journey of 13¼ miles was supposed to take just 32 minutes. Mine took a little longer.

Brixton is not a pretty sight. It is, as one would imagine, the scene of serious inner-city rioting would be, a collection of benefit offices and 'homeless units', with winos squatting at the street corners with their cans of beer. But this is also the location of a market which for years was the only place in the capital where you could rely on finding exotic produce such as pawpaws, yams and salt fish. Not surprising, when you consider that this is London's largest black neighbourhood. They say there is more widespread demand for this stuff than there is for haggis in Toronto.

But even Brixton has its moments. Like Upminster, Brixton has a windmill. There is even a sign directing visitors to this historic monument. It's not hard to find. You wander past The Windmill, a pub with guard dogs prowling the roof and, just behind the children's play park, it sits there with limp sails. There is no plaque giving any information. By contrast, a notice on the wee hut that serves as the children's play centre informs the locals that this is the Lambeth One o'Clock Club, 'for all adults with children under five'.

This is just off the main road, the A23, which carries signs for Brighton – only 49 miles away . . . the route travelled by the London to Brighton Car Run, no doubt, and Genevieve.

The prison is within sight. But London has twelve prisons, and one had been enough for me. I turned to make for the Tube and, choosing one of the six that deregulation made available for me, jumped on a London bus. I picked one in traditional red, with a platform and conductor, and bowled back down Brixton Hill to the station, re-living another London experience.

One of the few stops that I had determined to make was at Pimlico. There were two places here I wanted to see. In the one direction was the Tate Gallery, in the other Dolpin Square. I chose culture before gossip.

The Tate Gallery is founded on a collection of 70 paintings by Sir Henry Tate, the Mr Cube, you might say, of Tate and Lyle, the sugar refiners. The site of the gallery used to be occupied by Jeremy Bentham's Model Prison. Bentham, the nineteenth-century utilitarian philosopher, did rather well out of prisons. In his conception of the treatment of criminals, 'morals would be reformed, health preserved, industry invigorated, instruction diffused . . . ' – all by the construction of a 'Panopticon' which would allow the central supervision of convicts. After nearly 25 years of protracted discussions with the government, the plans were abandoned and Bentham, under a special Act of Parliament received £23,000. That was in 1813, when £23,000 would have bought a lot of Mars Bars.

The gallery building, opened in 1897, is a typical piece of Victorian excess – it's been likened to a wedding cake – but, untypically, because I consider myself a fan of the Victorians, I found it rather dull. But the collection is magnificent. They are all here: the movements, Pre-Raphaelites, French Impressionists, Cubists; the names, Turner, Gainsborough, Reynolds, Manet, Picasso, Matisse. I had visited the Tate once before, to view a Dali exhibition. On that occassion, I was so overwhelmed by the originality that he had added to his deft draughtsmanship that I bought a catalogue. Perusing it later, I discovered that the cover had been glued on upside-down. A surreal moment. On this particular visit, I could have spent the rest of the day with the Turners alone, but I had places to see.

Dolphin Square looks like a place rich in gossip. The largest block of flats in Europe, its 1,000 apartments house just under 4,000 tenants. They make an impressive list starting with the 23 peers and 59 MPs. A couple of years ago the list would have been headed by Mr and Mrs Tim Laurence – she used to be Mrs Mark Phillips. But either the traffic noise from the busy Embankment, the prostitutes who ply their lucrative trade outside or the cockroaches which recently plagued the buildings drove the Princess Royal back to Buckingham Palace.

So she can now be added to the equally impressive list of ex-tenants, including former Prime Minister Harold Wilson, former French President Charles de Gaulle, spy John Vassall, spyettes Christine Keeler and Mandy Rice-Davies, novelist C.P. Snow, world speed record holder Donald Campbell and Hubert Gregg. Hubert Gregg? You may not recognise the name but he is likely to make more of a lasting impact than any of the others because, in 1944, taking only 20 minutes, he wrote *'Maybe, It's Because I'm a Londoner'* in his flat in the Square. The royalties are still pouring in.

Victoria, from which the line takes its name, is the Underground's busiest station, handling a throughput of 80 million people and more than half the total number of passenger-journeys on the entire line. Victoria is, of course, the main line terminus for the south London suburbs and the wider reaches of southern England beyond – that great belt of richness from Kent to Hampshire which Northerners and Scots tend to denigrate, with justifiable envy.

Just off Victoria Street, which leads from Victoria station towards Parliament Square, is Westminster Cathedral. No, this is not Westminster Abbey, which is the one opposite the Houses of Parliament. Westminster Cathedral is the headquarters – or chief see – of the Roman Catholic Church in England and Wales.

Westminster Cathedral is one of those buildings that you need a post-graduate qualification in architecture to appreciate. It is odd-looking and a funny colour. In fact, it looks completely out-of-place. And that makes it ugly. But it can be explained. The architect was instructed to build something that could not be confused with Westminster Abbey, which, before being stolen at the time of the Reformation had been the cathedral of the one, true church. You then begin to understand why it was built in red and white brick. You appreciate that the architect, Bentley, mixed Romanesque and Byzantine influences, to give a Venetian effect . . . and you still think it is bloody awful. If the Catholic Archbishop who commissioned him wanted to differentiate it from its older rival, why did he not just pick a different name? You know . . . something really daring, like London Cathedral. And then Bentley could have designed a building more in keeping as a place of Christian worship, rather than something that could pass, in the dark, as an extension of the Topkapi Palace.

Its construction was completed only in 1903, although it really is still unfinished inside – despite some fine marble walls and glittering mosaics. Before the Cathedral was built, the site had a chequered history as a market and fairground, a maze, a bullring and a prison. Now, you can ascend the Campanile Tower to the four-sided viewing gallery which is 273 feet above ground level and offers spectacular views across London. It's much better value to make your way up here than to climb the 302 steps to get to the top of the Monument, when that is now dwarfed by the surrounding buildings.

There is an Underground connection here. One of the first visionaries to suggest an underground transport link for the centre of London was Charles Pearson, Solicitor to the City of London in the mid-nineteenth century. A liberal-minded person, Pearson was part of the successful campaign to have removed from the Monument the words that blamed Catholics for starting the Great Fire. They still couldn't become Monarch or Lord Chancellor. But they were no longer being blamed for burning the place down. The cathedral itself owes its present existence to that late Victorian liberal enlightenment which supported freedom of worship after 300 years of post-Reformation suspicion.

Until the building of the Victoria Line, Green Park was an insignificant stop on the Piccadilly Line. So what's upstairs? Well, Piccadilly, for a start, with all its elegant but faded Empire-style hotels. The station is located at the northern corner of Green Park, which is a large area of greensward and trees, criss-crossed with interesting footpaths but without the usual pond. It is much used by disrobing Londoners during the lunch intervals of hot summer days. The place is also overrun by rabbits.

Behind and under the massive and impersonal Green Park Hotel, down an alleyway off St James's Street, you might discover Pickering Place. It would literally be a discovery, for it is not on the A–Z map of London, and few people would venture there unless they knew where they were going. Pickering Place is, in fact, a bijou courtyard constructed in 1731. It is an architectural gem, and the location of the Texas Legation between 1842 and 1845, when Texas was an independent republic. A shiny brass (and astonishingly modern) plaque commemorates its past notability. It is, of course, actually modern, and made in San Antonio.

If you wander southwards through Green Park, you emerge five minutes or so later at the famous Queen Victoria monument at one end of Constitution Hill opposite Buckingham Palace. On major Royal occasions, the crowds used to be permitted to clamber all over Queen Victoria in order to get a better view of the palace balcony. Nowadays, it seems to act as a location for television camera platforms. Here, of course, is the centre of London tourism. Presumably for security reasons, there is no Underground station nearer than 1,000 yards away – though the Victoria Line carefully passes around Buckingham Palace and Queen Victoria at a depth of . . . well, I can't tell you because, before London Underground will disclose that information, you have to get security clearance. I filled in my form. But when I came to the question as to why I wanted the information I realised that despite my impeccable credentials, I would draw a blank. What was the point of satisfying them of my bona fides, if I was going to publish the data where it could be read by any old republican?

No foreign visitor leaves London without gazing at Buck House, which has been the London residence of the British monarch since Queen Victoria came to the throne in 1837. It has 600 rooms and is probably the most boring of all the royal palaces.

I have only been inside once, and I'm bursting to tell you about it. I hope that you won't think that I am boasting but it was when the Queen presented me with my CBE. I was Lord Lieutenant of Glasgow at the time and used to meet the Queen at least once a year. That year, she was in Glasgow in July, the day after I had been instructed to be at Buckingham Palace on the following 1 November, for the investiture. I told the Queen that I would certainly not forget the date, its being my birthday. Sure enough, come the day, as she placed the decoration round my neck she murmured 'Happy Birthday'. When I smiled, she added: 'See, I remembered.' What a pro!

Tottenham Hale and Blackhorse Road lie on either side of the River Lee, which meanders its way southwards to join the Thames at Canning Town, east of Blackwall, leaving a wide swathe of former marshland which must have flooded regularly in the time of the Romans. Nowadays, it acts as a ribbon of non-development, because the Victorians at least knew it would be foolish to build here, so unfounded would conventional foundations be. Instead, there are huge, shallow reservoirs, an essential part of London's water supply system. And these are flanked by numerous playing fields for sport and recreation. Nevertheless, the Underground goes under all this wetness, and presumably helps to reinforce the soggy soil like a steel rod in a concrete beam.

Walthamstow Central cannot be said to be anyone's idea of a tourist destination. But compared to Brixton, my starting point at the other end of the Victoria Line, it is slightly less run down. There is a high street market of the kind that in French ski resorts are considered quite good fun. Here, it is simply depressing, because of the cheapness of the goods on display.

In the 1970s, when local government was reorganised, the name of this part of Walthamstow became instantly famous when bureaucrats tried to imbue the newly created local authority with a spurious mediaeval cosiness which amounted simply to wishful thinking. Thus, Tower Hamlets Borough Council was born, trying to indicate a collection of attractive linked urban villages of great character. The reality, however, is that far from making progress to this unlikely Utopia, Walthamstow and the whole area has slumped further and further into characterless neglect. What a waste of an opportunity. How badly let down are the deserving citizens who live in Byron Road and Milton Street, in Church Hill and Rectory Road – all part of Tower Hamlets, five minutes walk from Walthamstow Central station.

Nevertheless, further north along Hoe Street to Forest Road, in the midst of this unpromising environment, there is an unexpected gem of an attraction for the visitor – the William Morris Gallery. Famous, of course, for his wallpapers and cotton prints, William Morris was one of the Victorian era's enigmas. He was vigorously opposed to modern civilisation, yet his own preferences paradoxically revolutionised the decorative arts tastes of his age and laid the foundations for modern design. His firm also produced furniture, textiles and tapestries, stained glass and ceramics. This collection of Morrisian genius is housed in Water House, a handsome eighteenth-century building which was Morris's childhood home for eight years. Morris's dilemma was that the works of art he produced were so costly that they were way beyond the pockets of ordinary folk: as a Socialist–idealist, this troubled him: 'I do not want art for the few,' he said, 'any more than I want education for the few or freedom for the few.' We are no nearer coming up with a solution to his philosophical problem, but maybe the products of Laura Ashley are an approximation to what he was seeking. Whatever your tastes may be, a visit to Water House is a rewarding end to a journey to the end of the Victoria Line.

After the depressing start at Brixton, my faith had been restored. It had turned out to be another good day on the Underground.

CHAPTER ELEVEN

THEN AND NOW

In recent years, London Underground chiefs have redrawn the familiar schematic map in different colours. They have announced and built new lines like the Victoria (light blue) and the Jubilee (mid-grey). But they've also given new identities to bits of old ones. Like the East London Line, which is orange, and the Hammersmith and City Line, which is a fetching shade of pink. I sometimes think the trains themselves should be painted the same colours as the map.

The Hammersmith and City Line is basically one branch of what used to be part of the Metropolitan Line. It goes as far as Aldgate East, but extends eastwards at peak hours along the District Line route to Barking.

There are two stations at Hammersmith. The main one, for the Piccadilly and District Lines, is big and modern and integrated with the brand new Broadway shopping mall. The station sparkles, and from it you can see the old-fashioned, yet, in many ways, more attractive, old station that serves as the starting point for the Hammersmith and City Line. Arriving there from Heathrow, I had begun to learn the hazards of travelling without a ticket, so I showed the one that I had purchased at the airport for transport to the city centre. 'It's valid,' pronounced the gateman. Otherwise, I might have discovered what promising career he had given up to move into this. Undertaking, if his sombre appearance was anything to go by.

On the brick wall of the station I could discern the remains of an old advert for the Hammersmith Palais de Danse. I don't know how this institution got into my consciousness, but there it certainly was, because the name was quite familiar. There must have been some programme or annual happening televised from it in the Fifties and Sixties (was it Miss World?), because the nostalgia remained.

The advert announced two sessions at the dance hall, three to six

in the afternoon for 2/6d and eight to 12 in the evening for 5/–. How
comfortable I felt with that money. I knew exactly how much it was,
instinctively. I could evaluate it and compare it and measure it. With
the decimal stuff I just pay it over. I really cannot *feel* how much
anything is costing me – even after 25 years.

It's the same with distance. Tell me it's half a mile, I'll be able to
judge how far and how long the journey might take. I feel I know.
Tell me it's 0.82 kilometres and you might as well be trying to tell
me in light-years. I find it particularly infuriating whenever I'm
asked on some official form or other for my own height or weight. I
know I'm five-foot-seven and eleven-stone-six. Tell me I'm one-
seventy and 72-point-58, and I'll presume you're talking about my
chest and waist measurements. In America, thank goodness, they
still stick doggedly to the old system, though they have shed the
stones. I can't begin to settle down to watch a boxing match from
Las Vegas without at least an attempt to divide the contestants'
weights by fourteen.

The advert carried what presumably was the Hammersmith
Palais' slogan 'The Talk of London'. Sadly no more. But it had been
in its day. In 1919, an enterprising Canadian, William Mitchell, saw
a site off Hammersmith Broadway and, according to the *Evening
News* of 22 October 1929, said to himself: 'I shall have the whole of
London dancing there in a few weeks.' Or: 'I shall make all London
dance just here', if you read to the end of the article. He attracted a
good deal of ridicule from people in the entertainment business, who
could see no demand for mass production in dancing. The 6,000 who
tried to get into the Palais on its opening night proved them wrong
and him right.

The trend towards public dancing had, in fact, started in 1912, but
World War I had brought it to a halt. Mitchell had realised this and
believed he could capitalise on it. He spent £30,000 converting the
old tramshed (which had also been pressed into service as an aircraft
hangar during the war) into a glittering ballroom, with Europe's first
custom-built sprung maple floor. Continuous music was provided by
a band at each end of the hall, one starting as soon as the other
stopped. There was a cage of instructresses who could be engaged as
partners for sixpence a dance. Male instructors were also available.
Formal dress was strictly adhered to, and the floor was protected by

insisting that the patrons changed into their dancing shoes.

Mitchell was a showman. He realised that the public wanted glamour. To a huge hall and superb floor he added a brilliant colour scheme and decor and scattered lots of little tables around for intimate tea and talk. But the thing he really invested in was the music. Mitchell went for the best, the best bands, the best musicians, the most flamboyant performers, presented in the most extravagant way. And in doing so not only created a rage for public dancing, but introduced jazz to the British public. On that first night in November 1919, the customers danced to the sounds of Billy Arnold's American Novelty Band and the Original Dixieland Jazz Band. When the music stopped at one end of the hall, 'it was renewed with thrilling vigour at the other'.

The ODJB was a quintet led by Nick La Rocca, a cornet player from New Orleans, who had already popularised jazz in the United States. Mitchell, albeit by default, gave him the opportunity to do the same in Europe. Nick La Rocca had been brought over to Britain in 1919 by the famous London impresario Albert De Courville, to appear in a revue at the London Hippodrome. But George Robey, the powerful star of the show, was so discomfited by the band's instant success that he insisted that they be dropped – which they were, after just one performance! Mitchell stepped in and signed them up for his new Palais, which was due to open in a few weeks, and they played there for nine months before going home triumphant.

The success of Hammersmith triggered a boom in dancing, and its format was copied all over London and the rest of Britain. The owners of the original Palais, in a celebratory first anniversary booklet, 'noticed with mingled feelings of pleasure and regret that several people have "lifted" the title of "Palais de Dance" as though it were the only title for a dance hall'. However, they were sure that 'the great general public is able to perceive the imitation from the real, to reject the tinsel when it is offered in place of the gold.

'The general public,' it went on, 'despises imitation, and every man and women with the financial ability to acquire it demands the genuine article.'

This souvenir booklet, which was presented free to patrons, also contains the most cloying appreciation of the boss that you are ever likely to read. Under the heading 'The Chief, Esteemed By All With

Whom He Comes In Contact', this eulogy consists of such phrases as 'from the lowest to the highest, no member of staff worked longer hours than he – nor is there one more zealous in promoting the success of the enterprises which he dignifies and which in turn assume a dignity of their own under his able direction'. He was 'the live wire of the dancing world that never fails to strike the point of contact with the general public'.

After such a sensational start, it is surprising to discover that the heyday of the Palais lasted only nine years. There were problems with the floor and there was the Depression. A new craze had come along – ice skating – and the Palais was converted into an ice rink. But that, too, lasted only until 1933 when it reverted to being a dance hall.

In 1938, it became the first ballroom to appear on television and, as changing trends forced it to drop its formality, it began to rediscover its popularity. World War II, with the restrictions on spending outlets for increased disposable income, meant that the Palais once again enjoyed a boom with servicemen of all nationalities. It was so famous that it even got a mention from Lord Haw-Haw.

Mitchell had prided himself on innovation, 'a man with an instinct for forecasting the trend of public taste and a wonderful capacity for knowing how to cater for it' – his souvenir booklet again.

In 1935, the Palais catered for one trend which was certainly ahead of its time – the Women's 'New Health' Movement for physical beauty and culture. Four sessions a day provided 'under ideal conditions' the opportunity 'to gain and maintain Perfect Health and Beauty'. And all for sixpence. The girl in the advert looks as thin as any of her Nineties counterparts. It was also nice to see the phone number given as RIVerside 0393. Do *you* remember WHItehall 1212?

Another first was the introduction in the 1960s of 'Sex Equality Dancing' for the first time in Britain – 'When West London girls ask you to dance' and 'Where men dare not refuse!' Men were encouraged to 'support your sex'. This daring offer was restricted to those of 23 years or over. By now the phone number had been changed to 01 748 2812.

This was the dance hall's golden age, first under bandleader Lou

185

LONDON LINES

Preager and then Joe Loss. But by the middle of the Eighties the dancing boom had finally played itself out – again. Another revamp was necessary. A £2 million facelift later, and the Palais became grammatically correct. It was Le Palais now, and a night club, billed as the World's Most Famous Nightspot.

I walked up Shepherd's Bush Road, looking for the famous Palais. I saw an old and ornate building, festooned with statues which I thought must be it. But it was the Hammersmith Library. The Palais is a much less impressive building, so anonymous that I had walked past it and missed it. The frontage looked sad and neglected, like a cinema turned bingo hall. I could see the corner of an old corrugated roof. It looked like a place that history had left behind.

Heading north on the Hammersmith & City Line is something of a sightseeing trip, because the line is not only not underground, but it is also well above ground – the views from its brick embankments offer a series of panoramas across west London which have their own interest.

It's easy to forget that this part of the 'Underground' system dates right back to just a year after the very beginning. The original line between Farringdon Street and Paddington, opened in 1863, was extended the following year to Hammersmith – not the present station, which was opened in 1868, but one a few hundred yards short. Indeed, in 1877, a little-known branch was opened via another station, Hammersmith Grove, which made a connection with the District Line at Ravenscourt Park (then known as Shaftesbury Road). This gave through access all the way to Richmond, which I would have thought was a connection worth making again. In fact, I wonder why it was disconnected at all?

The train pauses at Goldhawk Road, allowing you a glimpse of the open-air market which stretches down the street. Then the train clatters over the bridge, past where the BBC's Lime Grove television studios used to be, and more clatter over Uxbridge Road bridge to the high level Shepherd's Bush station. Onwards again, thundering past the impressive White City complex of the BBC Television Centre in a sweep which takes the line over Wood Lane. To the north, the silhouette of the White City Stadium, once an Olympic venue, then a dog track, now just another part of the BBC. Approaching Latimer Road (where there's another outdoor market), the train soars over the M41, connecting the permanent traffic snarls of Shepherd's Bush with the elevated Westway section of the A40(M) – so elevated that Ladbroke Grove, Westbourne Park and Royal Oak stations are completely overshadowed by the concrete monstrosity. Somehow, sitting in a train beside all this mayhem on the roads gives you a smug and satisfying feeling. I get the same feeling when travelling to London by train, looking out at the traffic on the adjacent M1 – apparently going backwards!

At Ladbroke Grove, I struggled to write down the name of the auctioneers who were selling off 'bits of London's history' – a sale of Underground memorabilia. I needn't have panicked. The ad was repeated at the next station, and the next, and the next.

The repetition worked. According to the auctioneers, the sale disposed of thousands of items; station signs, clocks, benches, loo signs and litter bins. A Bakerloo station sign went for £5, an Aldwych one for £250. But all of the advertising failed to move the train! For included in the auction was a four-carriage, 160-seater 1962 Central Line train. It had been hoped that it would fetch at least £10,000 from a theme park or a museum. But it failed to meet its reserve and was scrapped.

By now, the panoramas from my train had given way to unremitting views of endless stretches of brick retaining-walls as Paddington loomed. Beyond Paddington are the original 'cut and cover' tunnels of the first underground railway of 1863. My carriage of delight became just another in the endless stream of trains – District, Circle, Metropolitan, and even British Rail – serving stations out as far as Barking on tracks which are shared with the Hammersmith & City Line. It must be a pretty tricky task to timetable that lot.

I emerged at Edgware Road to check another location which has two different tube stations with the same name – the other two are Hammersmith and Shepherd's Bush, though you might have been forgiven for adding Charing Cross to the list, as I had already discovered.

I could see the purple heights of Hyde Park Mansions as we approached the station, and they loomed over it as I came out. They looked as if they were in the process of moving upmarket again after a period in the doldrums. But the improvements hadn't spread all the way round. Why they were painted in this extraordinary colour is anybody's guess. They would look much better in the traditional London cream and would complement the modern prosperity of Capital House, the local office block. Indeed, this was an area of some interesting design – the Metropole Hotel, with its external fire escapes and little brolly roofs, demanding attention.

Having ascertained that the Bakerloo Edgware Road was, indeed, a very short distance away, I returned to the Hammersmith & City station to resume my journey along this ancient line to Aldgate East.

It's a great Victorian creation, the Underground. They initiated, engineered and constructed the first parts of the system. They laid the foundations for a comprehensive transportation network which Londoners take completely for granted. But it's a creation of genius which continues to astonish visiting travellers like myself. It's beyond sensible valuation. But do we appreciate it? Maybe, if more of us used it, as I did, as a means of exploration, we would understand, and respect, both its origins and its future.

CHAPTER TWELVE

DOCKLANDS

One insurmountable problem I had in my attempts to complete my planned journey was that, through most of 1995, the East London Line was to be closed for modernisation. It was projected to be reopened by the end of October, so I left it till last. However, as the summer wore on it was clear that the timetable was slipping badly and eventually the reopening was indefinitely postponed. As a replacement service, buses had been laid on to run from Whitechapel to Wapping. But this didn't seem to me to be within the spirit of the journey. I might as well have taken a car along the route of the Central Line. So that was not an option. This, however, meant that I would not be able to visit that new symbol of London, the one that appears on telly whenever grim economic news – especially grim property price news – is being announced. I mean, of course, to the tower at Canary Wharf.

So eventually I decided to travel the Docklands Light Railway. I had misgivings about this as well because I am a literal, not to say pedantic, sort of a chap. This was supposed to be a journey on the Underground and the DLR is certainly not part of the Underground. But the area of London it covers seemed important, so I decided not to miss it out.

I wasn't too sure that I was going to like it. I didn't like the adverts attempting to get the passengers to call it the D. It is an ugly name and a bit forced. It reminds me of an attempt in the *Daily Mail* on D-day – the real one when we all went decimal. The reporter, desperate to find an angle on the story, purportedly went to some schoolyard and heard the kids referring to the new coins by nicknames, such as a 'lion' or a 'feather' or whatever was on the reverse/obverse/back of the new coins. Needless to say, that is the only reference to these names that has ever been seen.

I think D will have the same fate. The trick in doing this kind of thing is carefully to devise an attractive and believable name and to launch it with some appearance of genuine spontaneity. In other words, do what the Underground did with 'Tube', which people now think of as a nickname, but was in fact plastered on official signs outside the early deep stations. Why not 'The Doc'?

I arrived at Heathrow one Sunday morning, heading for The Doc, and received the only piece of misinformation that I ever got from Underground staff. I wanted to confirm that my £3.80 day ticket would cover The Doc, and the man at the ticket window told me that it was shut on a Sunday. There was, however, a bus service laid on, he said, from Bank. That left me with a big gap in my timetable. Eventually, I decided that I could reconnoitre the area by bus that day and come back and do it properly the next.

I had travelled very few Sundays on the Underground and, from this day's experience, I can tell you that it is not at its best on Sundays. It's the day that essential maintenance work takes place. This Sunday, chunks of the Northern and District Lines were out of action, and the Circle Line was shut altogether.

When I got to Bank, I went up to the little, fat smiling lady whom the Underground had thoughtfully told to wait for me at the top of an escalator. At least, so welcoming was she that it looked as though she had been sent especially to meet me. Of course, she hadn't been, because there was nothing official whatsoever about my travels. But so friendly and good at her job was she that she made everyone feel special. 'I know that the Docklands Light Railway' (I thought it was a bit too new to try out my nickname on her. No, not really. I hadn't thought it up yet) 'doesn't run on a Sunday, so can you tell me where I get the bus?'

'It doesn't run from *here* on a Sunday,' she said, 'I don't know why. They don't belong to us. They don't know what they're doing. It runs from Tower Gateway. Down to the District Line, one stop to Tower Hill, and you can pick it up there.'

And so I wandered through the vast city block that is the modernised Bank station. Passing the closed platforms of The Doc, after a long, long walk, I found the District Line and got to Tower Hill. Here the DLR is not integrated with the Undergound. You have to walk to another station, which they call Tower Gateway – it was the original western terminus. I also found out that The Doc had, indeed, not been running on Sundays for a considerable time because – despite its relative youth – it was being converted to a new Canadian-designed computer-based control system. The old (British) one, it seemed, would not cope with the more frequent trains and extended track system.

Now, the trains were running again on Sundays (though not yet to Bank). They run completely automatically, no drivers, just a series of 'interfaces' between the trains and trackside sensors connected to central computers. There are two of them, you and I might be reassured to know. They exchange information with the onboard computers on the trains at least once a second. And if they don't 'agree' with each other within three seconds, the rogue train is brought to a halt for safety reasons. I was reassured, too, to learn that there are actually a few human beings in the central control room, from where they can speak to passengers on platforms at any of the stations. A one-way communication, though.

After the confusion at Heathrow, I thought that I had better check that my ticket did indeed cover The Doc. The woman in the information booth at Tower Gateway confirmed that it did. But when I asked her how to get to Beckton she said, in a prim, defensive sort of way, 'We don't go to Beckton on a Sunday. We never have.' 'Where do we go?' I asked, mimicking her first person plural. But she wasn't going to smile at that.

It may have been all the months travelling underground, but The Doc was a mildly shocking new experience. From the station, I could see that the track was elevated. After Westferry, I could see it curving upwards like a rollercoaster in a most unpleasant, vertigo-inducing way. I longed for the security of the tubes.

I think it was really a feeling of guilt about using this alien system, but I was very picky about everything on the Docklands Light Railway. I hadn't much liked the woman at Tower Gateway. Now I didn't like the way the conductor/ticket-collector tapped one of the passengers on the shoulder to see his ticket. Underground staff wouldn't do that. I also thought that the whole system was a bit of a toy town railway. The trains were very short (two or three carriages). They were very slow. And the distance between some of the stations was minute. It takes only 40 seconds to travel from Canary Wharf to

Heron Quays. It takes even less time moving the other way, from Canary Wharf to West India Quay.

And the colours don't match. The official colours shown on notice-boards and station signs are a Miami Dolphin green and grey, while the livery of the trains is red, white and blue. The clash is harsh and discordant.

I was now on my way to Island Gardens, which sounded like a great place to go on a Sunday, a sort of combination of Coney Island and Tivoli Gardens. Sadly, the best thing about it is the name. I wasn't expecting an island, in this part of London none of the islands are. But I did expect gardens or at least some organised leisure activities. But there weren't any at all. Well, there were a couple of stalls selling Wall's ice cream, but I don't think you can count that.

I read the plaque that commemorated the opening of the railway by the Queen in 1987. I hadn't realised that it was that old. And then I followed the signs to the Greenwich Foot Tunnel, which I didn't know existed but was delighted to discover. There used to be a pedestrian tunnel under the Clyde in Glasgow, but that shut maybe 20 years ago. One of the rotundas which served as access to the tunnel is now a restaurant, the other is empty.

The Greenwich tunnel, opened in 1902, cost £127,000 to build. It is 1,217 feet long and is lined with 200,000 white, glazed tiles. It is 44 feet deep at Island Gardens and 50 feet deep at Greenwich. It is also 33 feet under water at low tide and 55 feet under water at high tide. As I read this going down in the lift, for some irrational reason it made me nervous. Irrational, because if the roof fell in, the amount of water that fell in with it would be academic. But I feel the same way in 'planes. Thirty-five thousand feet is much more scary than 22,000.

The lift, however, was modern enough for comfort having been installed in 1992 to replace the original one which had dated from 1904. The tunnel was busy with pedestrians and cyclists. All of the cyclists were pushing their bikes with their arms rather than their legs. They had been well warned in the lift. Lift operators would refuse to carry anyone caught riding a bike in the tunnel.

I was happy to discover the tunnel, because my failure thus far to visit Greenwich had been bothering me. It was not near any Tube station and thus did not afford easy access. On the other hand, it is in a very real sense where time begins and, particularly this close to a new millennium, I reckoned I was obliged to check it out. It hadn't seemed possible until now.

I set off with eager step to get through the tunnel. Well into the walk, I heard music but could not trace the source of it. A good while later, I came upon a busking guitarist. The tunnel really made the sound travel. As I walked on, I counted the steps. I could hear him from 50 paces away.

It was a great surprise to emerge and see the Clyde-built *Cutty Sark* dominating the view. I felt I was in the middle of the London Marathon. But, of course, you keep getting these surprises in London. The views are so familiar that, paradoxically, you're surprised when you chance across them, because the setting or scale aren't quite as you envisaged them. Incidentally, the motto on the back of the ship is 'Where there's a will, there's a way' – a bit twee, surely, for a ship that could cover 360 miles in a day? The Old Royal Observatory, the Royal Naval College and the National Maritime Museum are a marvellous architectural montage and made the whole long walk worth while.

But Greenwich itself is a disappointment. It was the only touristy area of London that I could say struck me as dirty. The buildings were peeling and the Chinese and Indian restaurants looked distinctly grotty. The packed Admiral Hardy pub was passable. But out the back was another of these markets with dozens of stalls selling junk. This one's speciality seemed to be pressed flowers. You could get them any way you liked. A favourite seemed to be a paper weight with 'For You, Grandmother' done out in leaves. Awful.

Across the road, in the window of Cassidy's Gallery, was a large print in a dirty wooden frame of the well-known painting of the two dogs called Dignity and Impudence sitting in a kennel. When I was ten, I had thought that this was pretty meaningful and witty. Now it just seemed trite. But it was an antique, no doubt about it. Because beside it was a rude notice in four languages. The English one read: 'We do not sell modern reproduction crap, only genuine antiques.' The other languages didn't seem to translate into anything as rude if my efforts at translating the Italian and Spanish were even half accurate. I tried to go inside to check just how genuine the goods were, but the shop was shut. So it didn't really matter what they were selling.

193

I walked back to the tunnel in search of *Gypsy Moth*, which I realised I had missed. I never found it. There was an empty concrete dry dock that looked about the right size, so I guess it was off on another tour round the world.

As I went in to the access building to descend into the tunnel, I could see its companion on the opposite bank. Just like Glasgow's, the two were of distinctly different design. In fact, a number of the old buildings that were still standing were reminiscent of those along the Clyde. I could identify, to give just one other example, a pump house from where fresh water used to be pumped on to ships. Back down the spiral stairs to the foot tunnel, I soon picked up the sound of the music again. Again, I counted my steps. As I approached the musician I realised that I had counted beyond 60. Surely sound didn't travel faster downhill! Then I noticed that he had been joined by another guitarist. Silly me.

The elevated station at Island Gardens is accessed by stairs and a lift. I thought I should try out the latter. It was the slowest lift I have ever been in. Fortunately inside there is a notice indicating that speed has been sacrificed for smoothness and that the journey would take longer than you might expect. Thank goodness for the warning, otherwise I would have thought that I had been trapped inside. But this station won't be here for too long. Before the end of the millennium, a new Island Gardens station will have been built – underground, as part of the £100 million extension of The Doc under the Thames to Lewisham. So The Doc will be underground, after all. I felt more comfortable about including the line in my travels. The extra stations include Cutty Sark (though I was told this might not be built unless privately–financed) and Greenwich – so it will be possible, at last, to visit the magnificent Nash buildings by train. I'm convinced it will be a very popular route for tourists.

The Doc's track system is in the form of a cross, and I was at the southernmost part of the system. I decided to travel all the way to the other end of the south–north line, to Stratford. After Poplar, the line quickly descended to ground level and became just a suburban railway. Arriving at Stratford, I remembered it from the Central Line and decided not to get depressed by staying, so I returned to Tower Gateway. I know that I should have got off at least one or two of the intervening stations like Bow Church or All Saints, both highly

194

appropriate for a Sunday, but I couldn't convince myself that this had anything to do with Docklands, which was what I was supposed to be looking at.

In its early days, the redevelopment of London's Docklands was the subject of much newspaper knocking. Sundry financial scams and scandals were uncovered as evidence of people achieving either fast bucks or faster bankruptcy. Now, practically all of Britain's national newspapers are produced from London's Docklands. It's amazing how quickly an area's fortunes can change. The movement of cargo through this area actually peaked as recently as 1961. Then, suddenly, everything shifted. The dockers had effectively priced themselves out of their jobs, unaware of the technological change which mechanised the industry at container sites like Tilbury, down the river.

Thus was born the London Docklands Development Corporation, charged in 1981 with the economic and social regeneration of eight and a half square miles from Tower Bridge to Woolwich. With the help of a ten-year-long Enterprise Zone offering tax breaks and other incentives, it is astonishing what has been achieved. Along the way, wharves which were difficult to sell for £90,000 in 1970 were fetching £6 million less than 20 years later. The value of land sold at £300,000 in 1983 multiplied tenfold within five years. In total £6.1 billion of private investment has been shoe-horned into the area by government investment of £1.7 billion – not a bad return. And the population has doubled.

As in any development, the transport infrastructure was vital. It was to be based on the new City Airport, brand-new four-lane highways – and The Doc. But it's the latter which has enjoyed spectacular success, much to the surprise of its early detractors. As its development caught up with the rest of Docklands, its original handling capacity of 1,800 passengers an hour has risen today to 24,000 passengers an hour – a dedicated railway which the 65,000 residents – 40 per cent of them owner–occupiers – have taken to their hearts. It's been a social revolution, created by a partnership between government and private finance. That's how we got the *Glasgow's Miles Better* campaign off the ground, so I have to approve.

On the Monday, Bank was open. The long, hot 1995 summer was continuing well into October. The temperature was in the high 70s, but it seemed much more pleasant than it had earlier in the summer. It took me some time to work out the difference, but I concluded that it was much fresher, less humid and oppressive at this time of year. Ideal travel weather. I could walk miles in this.

Coming into Shadwell, I noticed what looked like a high art-deco tower being renovated. On closer inspection it was the central well, stairway and lift shaft of a tower block. All of the flats which had clung to it had been demolished, presumably to be rebuilt. It looked much better as it was.

Today my plan was to travel to the farthest east of the Doc, to Beckton. To do that, I had to shunt into West India station and change trains, a rather awkward arrangement, but there is no direct route east. Having achieved this manoeuvre, I got off at the next station, Poplar, to have my first close look at the Canary Wharf Tower. It looked magnificent, gleaming so brightly in the sunlight that I had to squint to see it. Lucifer sprung to mind. All the main Canary Wharf buildings were plainly on view from here and the sight was impressive. It was a joy to walk back and forward across the station bridge admiring its construction of metal and glass. We really can still do some things very well. No wonder it was this area that the IRA targetted to end its ceasefire. It is the symbol of the London of the future.

I walked east along the busy road to the new Billingsgate fish market. I wanted to get in to nose around, but a forbiddingly high metal paling fence deterred me. The slight smell of fish on the wind didn't help either. In the car park I could see at least one red Porsche, so some people are still doing well out of fish. Just past the market is the most modern of McDonald's. Now you will have your own views on fast food, but you have to concede that when this particular chain wants to go into an environmentally-sensitive area, they do make an effort. This particular restaurant must have won an architectural award. Fortunately it was just too early for lunch, otherwise I would have been tempted to put on a couple of thousand calories.

Just at East India station is another dramatic building. Curiously, for such an impressive structure, it had no visible identifying marks.

I had to walk all the way up to the security guard to discover that it was Reuters, and I remembered that they were said to be the last journalists to leave Fleet Street (the blinkered metropolitan press had ignored D. C. Thomson's Dundee papers). I was able to have a closer look at a curious little structure. It was like the cooling tower of a mini-power station – maybe that is what it was, because it was churning away nineteen to the dozen.

Virtually under the station stairway there is a large pool covered with what looks like green slime which ducks were gliding over. On closer inspection, I could see that it was not slime but weeds, indicating not pollution but clean water. Many of Britain's canals have the same problem. Cleaning up the water allows weeds to grow which can then only be kept down by the movements of the boats.

At Royal Victoria station you can see the shapes of two gas-holders – what we used to call gasometers until purist cricket commentators broadcasting from the Oval corrected us. I say, 'you can see': in fact you can't miss them, because they are painted in the most garish blue and yellow with red and green pipes. I later discovered they were not gasometers at all, but the Royal Docks pumping station. Again, I have to compliment the architect. If you have to erect functional buildings, you might as well make a feature of them.

After trundling through Royal Victoria I began to appreciate how much land there is here. At once, it gives you an an idea of the true scale of London, because this is just a fraction of the city. And it is amazing to think that all of this was needed to handle the amount of cargo that came and went. No bare tonnage statistics can convey the impression of immensity that these deserted acres can. Work is going on, of course. For one thing, you can see the construction of the extension to the Jubilee Line. But there is a lot of land to fill, and it's going to take some huge amount of investment. Custom House is called after a tidy four-storey building on the river side of the tracks. Or is it after the bigger building on the other side, the one with the flying angel reading the book? What a show-off!

At Prince Regent, one of the few flour mills left standing thrusts its attention on you from among the devastation. This is Spillers millennium Mill, an odd or very futuristic name for something that must be a hundred years old. Looking out from here you can see still more derelict land. The confidence that the solidity of Canary Wharf instills enables you to envisage all the land filled with burgeoning new buildings. It will be done. And it won't be very long either.

Approaching Royal Albert there are signs of two different kinds of life. Out of one window are the allotments from a slower, simpler age. Out the other side is the City Airport. It seems a bit under-used still. There were three 'planes on the tarmac as I went out and only one on the way back. Starting here, too, was a full-length rowing course called Gallion's Reach, which ran on further than the next station. This place suddenly seeemed vaster than the Alaskan tundra.

As I sidled into Beckton I could see the remains of buildings that looked as if they had been blasted by Serb artillery or shelled by HMS *Belfast*, which evidently can take out anything within 14 miles of Tower Bridge.

The station at Beckton, like all of those on The Doc, was well laid out. It was made from clean-looking materials, frosted glass and a white brick floor. The railway seemed to be keeping its promise of customer care. But on this hot autumn day the only query I had was how pleasant these exposed, elevated stations would feel on a freezing windy February day. Then, I suspect, a bit of non-designer cover would be most welcome.

I didn't plan to waste much time in Beckton, just enough to confirm that there was nothing there. Well, there was nothing much. There was the Windsor House pub with its kiddies' playground, the BP filling station and the shopping centre and retail park, with the usual Curry's, Texas and so on. Fine, I thought, I could now get back on the train and head for Canary Wharf. But, walking up the stairs, I caught sight of a sign to Beckton Alps with a little walking figure. This is just the kind of trap I'd been falling into all summer, seeing something and, unplanned, on impulse, at the drop of a hat, diverting off to explore it. This is why I had painful feet. But I'd also had good fun. So, even now, trying to contain my demob happiness on this my last day of tubular travel, groaning that I had glanced up at the sign, I set off for the alps.

There they were, in Alpine Way E6, forming a dry ski slope. There was the Alpine café bar where I could bring my family for *après-ski* drinks, or the charming chalet-style Mountain restaurant with its excellent cuisine in a stylish and relaxed atmosphere. It even contained a function suite, the Aviemore Suite, named by people who obviously had never skied there. I do not like to talk my country down, but skiing in Scotland is the most miserable of experiences. It is cold, windy, wet. And that's just in the car park where most people slide into their sallopettes. Scotland can boast many visitor attractions, but it should stay out of the ski market. The simple fact is that the mountains are not high enough. I'm sorry but 3,000 and a bit feet are simply not enough to give good snow and long runs for sufficient days in the year. I didn't need the Beckton Alps to remind me of this. So it was a relief to discover that, despite adverts and notices to the contrary, all the restaurants were shut. Maybe *that's* why it's called after Aviemore.

On top of the slope there's a beacon, the Beckton beacon, I suppose. On this flat landscape, it was certainly the highest point for miles. There was nothing for it, I would have to climb to the top. The winding path was not especially gentle, but I got fed up zig-zagging and cut across a couple of corners to get up quickly. It was quite a view. The flat roofs of the industrial estate, the pylons supporting the roofs in the retail park as an attempt at variety, the 'plane taking off from the airport, a neat and modern football stadium which I took to be Upton Park and, in the distance, hills with a TV tower on top. It looked like Alexandra Palace, but my orienteering isn't good enough to confirm this. Anyway, it was a rare view back past Canary Wharf to the City, again emphasising the vastness of the docklands development. Normally when I am up this high, I make a point of skiing down. But, despite more notices to the contrary, the slope was as firmly shut as the café, not a hired boot in sight, so I just had to walk all the way back down.

'Next Train Island Gardens' according to the electronic sign. But in permanent black lettering below 'Check Front of Train for Destination'. I did. Where was 'Red Route'? Anyway, on this train set, you couldn't go far wrong and I was soon trundling into Canary Wharf.

I came down from the station into a really classy shopping mall. All the shops were good names, Jaegar, Austin Reed, Mondi, Blazer, Tesco. Yes, there really is one there, but I wasn't going to spoil the affluent atmosphere of the rest of the place by checking it out, though I am sure that it only sold deli products.

199

There was a totally American feel about the mall. Not just in its layout and the quality of its finish but in the young American male accents of the jacketless executives ordering pastrami on rye and bagels for their early lunch. I ordered a bagel, too, and took it out on to the marble piazza with its flowers, fountains and running water.

I was surrounded by beautiful buildings. This place had really been done properly. Each building in the square was different. There was no obvious symmetrical layout round the square. And each building was unique.

I walked down the few steps to ground level and was surprised to encounter London traffic. Arriving by train into a unit designed for pedestrians, it was easy to forget that this was still connected by road to the city. A Polish tour bus was sitting outside. Ten Cabot Square was a tall, clean structure whose corner windows reminded me more strongly of Boston than London. Opposite, 25 Cabot Square is a complete contrast – strong and commanding. A third structure, despite the fact that its off-white marble and blue glass exterior was not yet finished, looked brilliant, too. I walked out to Westferry Circus to have a look at the river, passing a red brick building, One Park Place, of much smaller scale. Surrounded by water, it fitted in, too.

Looking back at the place from the Thames, the only conclusion was: this works.

Most of the main streets were named after famous Englishmen, maritime explorers mostly, though Wren had crept in as well. But who was this Scot, MacKenzie? Then I remembered the river in Canada. Must be the same bloke.

I wandered back to have a look inside Canary Tower before moving on. One Canada Square – that appears to be its official name – has a huge entrance hall of opulent marble of red, black, white and grey and an aluminium ceiling. I walked through to the banks of lifts. I was going up to the top, until I heard one of the commissionaires telling another visitor that there were no public tours. So I wandered over to the 'Tenants Only' lifts and pressed the top floor. But they obviously weren't operational yet. So I got out again, looked at the tenancy board, and selected EuroTunnel on the twenty-ninth floor as an appropriately modern firm to visit. Even on that floor, there were empty offices which allowed me to have an uninterrupted view out over London. On the way down I noticed the unnerving wind up the lift shaft that you get in these high buildings. The Sears Tower in Chicago is the draughtiest, but even Doris Day knew that. I was glad to get out.

I then went on my way to Crossharbour to have a look at the Docklands Visitor Centre. There I watched the video, fronted by an ageing television face whom I couldn't identify until I started writing this. He was, of course, Desmond Wilcox – Esther Rantzen's husband. I missed the first few seconds so I don't know what his precise connection with the place was. But he obviously had one, because he was saying 'When I came back ten years later . . .'

The film gave an excellent overview of the development and the dislocation and readjustment that the decline of the docks had forced. We are talking about eight and a half square miles and something like 55 miles of water frontage. Mudchute Farm itself is 12 acres. Wandering around the exhibition I could put names to buildings that I had seen; Cascades, the futuristic flats on the Isle of Dogs, Canada Water wind pump, and the Royal Docks pumping station.

I walked back to South Quay unashamedly admiring everything, even the way the clock had been hung between the two parts of Meridian House. Lloyd's Bank looks like it is floating as freely as the Jumbo Restaurant in Aberdeen Harbour – Aberdeen, Hong Kong, that is. And at Heron Quays the offices have their own pontoons and docks. It was with horror, that only a few months later, I sat and saw on television the scale of the destruction caused by the IRA bombs to these beautiful buildings. What senseless waste.

I passed out of Docklands over the Big Top of Peter Jay's International Festival of Circus, past the anglers at their numbered stations at Limehouse and back to the real world and the Tube at Tower Gateway. Flying in to Glasgow airport a couple of hours later, I looked out at our own docklands, so much smaller and so much more derelict. I appreciated for the first time the comments of those critics who deplored the Scottish Exhibition and Conference Centre building – a vast red tin shed which covers the old Queen's Dock site in Glasgow. It would not have been used as a workman's hut in London's Docklands.

And so, once more, I was brought back to the fact that London has the confidence – and the financial clout – to do things properly. But I also remembered the investigation by a Scottish journalist into the funding of the Docklands regeneration, and how this amounted, in effect, to a massive subsidy to London by the whole nation. Why not? After all, it is the capital city.

CHAPTER THIRTEEN

FATHER OF THE MAN

By the fairly straight-forward method of contacting one of my old school pals, I had discovered the London address where I had stayed 39 years ago – Duncan Terrace. Looking it up on the map, I discovered that it was only a couple of hundred yards from the Angel tube station. So I kept it for my last, special, journey.

I had been in the Angel before as I explored the Northern Line. But this time I was looking for signs to trigger off my memory. There was certainly nothing in the station that would do that. It had been thoroughly modernised.

I orientated myself at the crossroads and turned down City Road. First left was Duncan Terrace. I walked along the terrace, not recognising the green shrubbery that ran the whole of one side. I had not been given the number of the house, but had assumed that I could easily locate the spot where, all those years ago, I had dropped the keys down a drain.

The most likely place seemed to be at the corner of the terrace and Duncan Street. There indeed was a drain. And there was a plaque on the pavement beside it. I expected it to read 'Here, on Whit Monday 1954, Michael Kelly, while yet a boy, dropped the house keys down this drain'. Instead, it rather disappointingly proclaimed 'Towpath Link, Islington Tunnel, Regent's Canal'. Evidently, Regent's Canal ran all the way under Duncan Street to Caledonian Road. And it had been doing so since long before 1954.

I tried to imagine the day that the Corporation cleansing truck had turned the corner and rescued me. But, thinking about it that night, I couldn't get the direction of the truck right. I clearly remembered its making a left turn into the street that I stood in. The way I had worked it out today, the truck would have had to have turned right. What had not seemed particularly important a few months ago, assumed a ridiculous significance. Not that it really mattered one way or the other. But it would be satisfying if I could confirm how many of my memories over those 39 years had been accurate.

Obsessed now, I returned to Scotland determined to trace the man whose keys I had lost. My first task was to track down my old headmaster, Brother Gall, a surprisingly easy job through the sophisticated network of the Catholic church. I did not, however, expect to find him living 300 yards from my own home in Glasgow.

I phoned him up. He remembered me.

'Can you help me find the man who ran the house in Islington in 1954?' I asked him.

'That's not difficult,'he replied, 'he lives here too. He's Brother Peter.'

Brother Peter came to the phone. 'Brother,' I began, 'do you remember when a group of us came down to Duncan Terrace on our way to Rome?'

'Yes,' he said, 'and you dropped the keys down a stank.'

I was flabbergasted. He was now well over 80. It had been an important incident in my young life, but how could he still remember it?

'Listen,' he said, 'if you knew how vital those keys were to the running of the house, you would know how I remember. I just had to get them back.'

Evidently, the key ring had held a number of unique keys and he himself had walked to the council offices and persuaded them to send what he called a 'gulley sucker' to clear the drain. The house was Number 46 and the drain had been right outside the door.

But why had I been given the keys? His story was that another boy had injured his foot on the journey down from Dumfries, where our school was, and had been told to rest to give him every chance to travel on to Rome. When the other boys were leaving for their tour of London, I had volunteered to stay and keep him company, because I had seen London before. He had always remembered it as a kind Christian act.

It didn't sound like me at all. I am sure that I had never been in London before that visit. My mother, in her nineties but still *compos mentis*, confirmed this. My guess is that, after a night without sleep on the train down, I simply did not fancy trailing about London in a bus which I knew would make me travel sick. I had used my injured pal as a good excuse.

But that still didn't explain why I was standing outside the house with this big bunch of keys. And there is no use worrying about it any longer. I'll never know now.

Before I went back to the Tube for the last time, I walked about a bit thinking about my tubular trips. It had been great fun. I would recommend it to anyone. The Underground is so vast, and the choice of stations so wide, that I could come up with a wholly different set of experiences if I were to start again. For example, I hadn't been on the Tube to a football match, or during Christmas shopping, or to theatreland, or to the café in the crypt of St Martin's-in-the-Fields. I hadn't seen Pinner, or the Boat Race, or Hatton Gardens, or kite–flying on Parliament Hill, or polo. I hadn't watched Middlesex play cricket at Uxbridge, or the Changing of the Guard, or the Ceremony of the Keys, or the Trooping of the Colour. I hadn't visited Bleeding Heart Yard, or Friday Hill, or the Public Records Office. I hadn't played golf on any one of countless courses, or joined the Notting Hill Carnival, or scented the Chelsea Flower Show, or eaten in Chinatown.

I hadn't even seen the statue of Charles I in Whitehall, which an enterprising brazier, John Rivett(!), bought from Cromwell to melt down. He made a fortune selling brass trinkets, until sanity and the monarchy were restored. He then produced the statue, whole and entire, and sold it back to Charles II for £1,600.

I hadn't seen the Reform Club, from where Phileas Fogg left, allegedly returning 80 days later. And I hadn't been to 84 Charing Cross Road.

But I had seen plenty. And I was now a confirmed Tube fan. If any of the world's other 88 cities that boast an underground system have a better one than this, I would like to see it. Commuters may hate the congestion, they may be irritated by breakdowns and delays. But this system works. And it is staffed by properly trained personnel. I don't just mean the drivers, who are obviously skilled at the job they do. I mean the attitude and approach of the staff generally.

True, no one I had to ask for help matched the romance of the British Rail hostess on the Cardiff to Paddington Express some years earlier. In answer to a fairly straightforward question about who lived in a big, tree-shrouded house on the banks of the Thames near Windsor, she quoted at me, 'We are neither wholly bad or good, Who have our lives here in this wood'. But then she was Welsh.

London Underground clearly invests in its people, because they are polite, caring and knowledgeable.

I had also changed my attitude to London. Before, it was an obstacle to be overcome, a morass to struggle through in order to conduct necessary business. It was also an alien, if not a foreign, place. Now, I see it as a great international city. Stately, beautiful, infinitely varied. I also see it as the capital of Great Britain. If Scots have a problem with it seeing it as English and insular, then it is symptomatic of something wrong with us.

In its grandeur, it does manage to epitomise Britain's history and heroism. The standards, the stance for democracy, the tolerance and, not so much the will to win, but the bloody–mindedness not to lose.

I also learned to enjoy Londoners. I don't remember a single occasion when anyone took the initiative to speak to me. But when I spoke to them – to ask for change, to get directions, seeking local information – they were, without exception, friendly and helpful. Often, I thought they were just happy to be asked, as if few people ever did ask them anything.

If I were to contrast them with Glaswegians, then I would say that the Glaswegian is always trying to be friendly, determined to live up to that image, as if to compensate for the perceived deficiences of his home town, but without the confidence just to let it happen. Londoners have a confidence which they acquire from their city.

As I wandered about Islington that wet, autumn evening – walking through the rain that is supposed to be so typical of London yet had been absent for seven long months – I tried to experience the changes that must have taken place over the four decades since my very first visit.

To take just one thing, just look at the shops. There wouldn't have been a Generous George's fast food restaurant. There wouldn't have been a shop converted to the Islington Museum. There wouldn't have been a charity shop selling clothes to raise money for famine relief abroad. There wouldn't have been wine bars, or a Tennessee Fried Chicken or a Chinese or Korean restaurant or a Christmas shop or a health food shop. There wouldn't have been a Tanerife Tanning salon or a Wrought Iron Shop.

And, further along Holloway Road, just across from the Tube station, there wouldn't have been the main campus of the University of North London.